# MASTER ENGLISH FAST

## AN UNCOMMON GUIDE TO SPEAKING EXTRAORDINARY ENGLISH

## DR JULIAN NORTHBROOK

# CONTENTS

## COMPLETE AUDIO VERSION
## OF THE BOOK

THE BEST LEARNING happens by consuming the same information multiple times, and in multiple formats.

To help you with this, I've included a complete audio version of this book (as long as you have a smartphone that can use the "Learnistic" app).

Instructions for getting this can be found in the "Some Free Resources" section at the back of the book.

Important: the audiobook is only available via the Doing English Learnistic app, so if you don't have a smartphone this will be unavailable to you.

## PREFACE

Welcome to *Master English FAST: An uncommon guide to speaking extraordinary English.*

And welcome to my extraordinary world.

I'm Dr Julian Northbrook, and by making the effort to get this book in your hands you've taken the first step to mastering English. More about me in a moment.

This book is intended to be a broad overview of all the things you need to know to improve your English as a high-level—but stuck, and probably really bloody frustrated—speaker of English as a second language.

First, a warning: **If you don't really need English in your life, if you aren't motivated, or if you are lazy and you can't take tough advice, this book is not for you**. Stop reading right now and go watch TV instead.

Don't waste your time; I know I don't want to waste mine.

The methods you'll learn here work. But they may seem unconventional. For example, do you believe that the most important thing is to memorise more vocabulary words? That you must practise with native speakers to get good at English? Or that just listening can get you fluent? All of these common beliefs are very, very wrong.

To benefit from this book, you must be willing to let go of your assumptions. If you're not willing to listen, and if you don't want to change your own (probably false) opinions, stop reading right now.

This will require hard work. There is no free lunch, as the saying goes – meaning that nothing comes without a price. If you want to master the English language, you must be willing to do the work. If you are lazy, if you are satisfied with half-assed efforts and mediocre results, stop reading right now, please.

As you've probably noticed by now, I am frank, outspoken, and don't care if I upset you by telling you the truth you need to hear.

This book is for people who are tough. People who can listen to criticism. People who can get angry and then use that energy to work harder instead of just giving up (again).

You must be willing to look in the mirror and admit that you don't like what you see; you have to be willing to change your bad habits and make difficult choices.

You have to sort out your priorities, recognise what's most important to you, and be willing to make the necessary sacrifices. If you are sensitive, if you get easily offended, if you tend to quit when the going gets tough, please, for the love of God! Stop reading this book right now!

One more thing: I have absolutely no problem with "bad" language. I swear in my day-to-day conversation. And I'm not afraid to use words like shit, fuck and even on occasion when it suits me, cunt. These words exist in the English language for a reason – they convey emotions that normal words can't. I have no intention of changing the way I speak for anybody, so if this offends you? Just don't read this book!

All this said, here's my promise to you: if you are willing to let go of your assumptions, listen to my advice and do the bloody work, this book will get you started on the right path to speaking the extraordinary

English you need and becoming the extraordinary person you know you can be.

Sound good?

Good.

With that, let's get this show on the road.

———

Want a free gift from me?

If you find a typo, error or spelling mistake in this book: email me at julian@doingenglish.com to let me know – if I haven't already found and fixed it, I'll send you a small something as a thank you.

## INTRODUCTION

In the summer of 2007, I got on a plane bound for Tokyo, Japan.

I had a job interview lined up for a great position at an art gallery in Harajuku, a fashionable part of the city. I felt sure life was going to be awesome.

Only it wasn't.

I got turned down for the job.

Why?

Quite simply, because my Japanese was _crap_. I was fully qualified in art and had everything the gallery needed – apart from the fact that I spoke Japanese like a two-year-old with mental health problems.

From there I suffered three long, painful years feeling embarrassed about my poor language skills, feeling stupid every time I spoke, and frustrated as hell because I just didn't know what to do in order to improve.

Eventually, I worked out what I was doing wrong and mastered the language—I'll share all of that, and more, with you in this book—, but the journey there was a long, painful one.

### *The Day I Forgot Japanese Wasn't My First Language*

I'll never forget the day I realised I'd done it. The day I realised I'd overcome my language problems and mastered Japanese.

At 10 am I stepped off the cool, air-conditioned coach into a hot and humid train station car park. I was at a train station somewhere in Ibaraki, Japan – in the middle of nowhere.

The car park was empty.

Looking towards the station I saw no trains – a very different sight to the station near my home in Tokyo, where trains go in and out every few seconds. I was doing research at a private secondary school in the area, and I'd gotten on a coach early that morning to get there. Someone was going to pick me up by car at 11 am, but by chance I'd caught an earlier bus and arrived almost an hour ahead of time.

Not too sure what to do, I looked around.

In the corner of the station car park, there was a tiny wooden building. It looked like a garden shed, raised up on a platform. There were some steps leading up to the wooden platform where a small plastic table and two plastic chairs were set. Right next to the chairs there is a sign: *"Ice Coffee – 150 yen"*.

Well, there's no point in standing around in the heat for an hour, I decided. So I climbed little wooden steps to get a coffee.

Was anyone even there, I wondered.

*"Konnichiwa!"* I called out.

The door opened, and a lady probably in her 50s came out.

She froze, stunned.

I'm quite used to this in Japan. A lot of people get nervous around English speakers – a result of failing to learn any kind of practical English at school. And this is especially true in the countryside, where you rarely see foreigners.

I pointed at the sign and asked for an iced coffee in Japanese. She looked relieved. *"You speak Japanese?"* she asked.

*"Just a little,"* I replied. *"I'm still studying and not very good yet."*

That was a lie. I'd already passed the highest level of the Japanese Proficiency exam, worked as a freelance translator, and was currently the headteacher at a Japanese company dealing in business-to-business English programmes. *(Why I said "I'm not very good yet" will become evident later in this book.)*

She got me my ice coffee and motioned for me to sit at the little plastic table next to the door.

For a few seconds, we were both silent.

Then she started to talk.

Sitting in her shed all day, she apparently didn't have much to do. So she killed time reading books and magazines. And she had *a lot* of interesting things to talk about. She told me all about the history of the area. Apparently, nearby was a shrine that had been established in 600 BC, and the town was also the birthplace of *Juri Takahashi*, one of the members of the girl-band AKB48.

Have you ever been so engaged in a conversation that you completely forget everything around you?

It's like the rest of the world disappears, and time flows on without your noticing.

It seemed like I'd only been there a few seconds when my phone rang.

*"Hey, I'm here,"* said my friend with the car.

An entire hour had already passed!

Saying goodbye, I left the cafe and ran over to my friend's car. I got in and said hello (in English). I said that I'd arrived early, but it was OK, because I had enjoyed having a coffee and a chat with the lady in the cafe.

This friend is someone I always speak English with, so it wasn't strange when he asked, *"Oh? She could speak English?"*

The realisation happened *right then.*

*"Er… I'm not sure."* I said.

What language had we been speaking? I couldn't remember. I'd been so absorbed in the conversation that I wasn't aware of what language we were speaking. Logically, I knew it must have been Japanese, but I'd been totally unconscious of the fact.

That's the moment I knew I'd made it.

*I'd forgotten Japanese wasn't my first language.*

And that is <u>exactly</u> the kind of moment I want to help you experience in English.

### Welcome to the First Day of the Rest of Your Life

By opening this book, you've made a life-changing decision. You're here with this book in your hands because your English skills hold you back and stops you being the person you want to be and living the life you want to live.

I understand: *I've been there.*

This book is going to give you the quick 'n' dirty lowdown on improving your English as a high-intermediate to advanced speaker.

Whether you're a freelancer, an artist, a translator or a writer, a business owner, a businessman, an executive, you live in an English-speaking country or you teach English as a second language—and I've been all of those things—you feel frustrated by your English.

You know that improving your English skills will make your life better…but you don't know how to do it. Well, it's a mistake to think you can do the same things as you did when you were a beginner in English. As soon as you hit the intermediate level, everything changed, including the things you need to do in order to improve.

### Who the Hell is Dr Julian Northbrook?

Hi. I'm Dr Julian Northbrook.

And yes, I am a real doctor.

But please, don't come to me with a heart attack or other medical emergency – I'm not THAT kind of doctor.

More importantly, why should you listen to me?

Well, I could tell you all about my extensive experience teaching and coaching people to speaking amazing English, about my master's degree in Applied Linguistics (with distinction, no less) or my PhD research in second-language acquisition and the publications I have in top academic journals. I *could* tell you all about those things, but I won't, because nobody gives a shit about those qualifications.

What I will tell you about, though, is this – *the pain I experienced while learning my second language.*

You see, there are far, far too many language teachers in the world who have either never learned a second language themselves, or have never taken it past the low-intermediate stage.

Should you trust these people?

I say no.

I mean, I certainly wouldn't.

Just like I wouldn't trust a music teacher who couldn't play music, a hairdresser with dirty hair or a dentist with bad teeth.

In my opinion, the best way to measure a teacher's ability to help you is not by the qualifications they can list, but rather by the number of hours they've spent struggling in a second language themselves.

Well, I've spent *many* hours struggling.

If you want to know more about my story, I've written about it at length here: https://doingenglish.com/about.

## CHAPTER 1
## WHY YOUR ENGLISH SUCKS

WHEN I LEFT my full-time secondary school teaching job in 2014, I went from standing up all day long teaching classes to sitting in front of the computer all day. But I didn't change my diet at all… on the contrary, because I was at home I started snacking all day, and drinking more in the evenings.

You can guess what happened next, right?

Yes, I got fat.

So I got a personal trainer – Phil (also known as 'Phil the Cunt', for reasons that would be very clear if you ever worked with him). Well, when I started working with Phil, the last thing I wanted to do was diet and work out. I just wanted the results…*fast*.

Most people don't do anything until it's too painful not to. Me included. When I started working with Phil, I did so because I'd gotten unhealthy and overweight. My stomach was hanging over my belt, and I had very little energy. I wanted results...*yesterday!*

We live in a world where everybody wants everything instantly, and without effort.

A magic pill that makes them fluent in English.

A button to push that magically makes them speak without making embarrassing mistakes.

I'll tell you now: just like there is no magic fitness fix, there is no instant method for mastering English, either.

This said, it only took me two months of dieting and working out with Phil to get back into shape, which is pretty damn fast.

The reason I tell you this is because the thing that made the biggest difference to me was the way Phil corrected me on some false beliefs.

So that's why I'm going to start with the same thing as Phil did with me: by changing your mind about a few things.

There is no quick, instant method to master English. It's always going to take dedication and hard work. But there is one thing you can do right now to begin improving faster – *fix the way you think.*

My friend Hitomi Horiguchi (a life-coach I know in Tokyo) very rightly says, *"If you fix your thinking, then your actions will also change."*

Very true words.

Here's a great example from Gilda, one of my recent "Master English *FAST* Accelerator" coaching course graduates:

---

 *"Not only have I got amazing insights into how the brain of a learner works which has allowed me to create much more effective lessons, but I've experienced a shift in my mindset. Julian has helped me turn my 'flaws' into my success. and I know from now on it can only be better."*

---

Gilda is also an English teacher, teaching in Italy. And though English is not her first language, she was already very fluent when she joined my course.

For her, the problems she needed to fix were largely to do with her attitudes and beliefs – things like, *"I can never be as good as native speakers as an English teacher"* (which simply isn't true). And because of these beliefs, she didn't take all the opportunities that came her way. Or use many of the things she personally has to benefit her students that native speakers don't have – like her deep knowledge of things Italian learners of English struggle with, and her own experience mastering English (remember: never trust an English teacher who had never mastered a second language themselves). As soon as we changed her mindset, the way she teaches and uses English in class changed too – i.e. her *actions* changed.

If you're interested in the MEFA course, and getting coached through the process of mastering English, check the back of this book where I've included information.

The point is, the way you think defines the way you act. When you make a mistake, it's easy to feel bad about it. But if you understand that mistakes are a part of the learning process, everything changes.

There are lots of reasons why your English might not improve… but in most cases, it comes down to a few very common problems. Most of them are to do with your mindset – the way you think about improving your English and then actually using English in the real world. You need to retrain those bad habits, otherwise they'll hold you back forever.

My goal in this book is to totally change the way you think about learning (and using) English forever. So, with that, let's dispel some myths...

### Reason 1: You Think You Can't Master English

Here's a dirty little secret: *I failed French when I was a student.*

You probably studied English at school, but being British, I studied French. And I *hated* those classes. It was all boring grammar exercises, copying from the textbook and translating sentences. I couldn't see any way that learning French was going to improve my life, and I didn't care whether I got good grades. But years later I had a chance to live in Switzerland for three months, all expenses paid. I turned it down because I wasn't confident enough to go to a French-speaking country. Suddenly, I could see how French might improve my life, but there was still one big problem: I didn't believe I *could* learn French!

Years after, I struggled with Japanese and believed it was because I wasn't talented at languages. Again, I had "the *Why*"—a real reason to learn Japanese—but I believed I couldn't do it.

*"Whether you think you can or you can't, you're right"* famously said Henry Ford. Whether you find a solution to your problems and do what it takes is largely defined by your attitude.

If I asked you, *"Can you fly?"* you'd probably say "no". But that's short-sighted and rather uncreative.

Imagine if the Wright brothers had done the same thing: *"Hey, Wright, can you fly?"* I ask.

*"Fly? No! Of course I can't – people can't fly!"* they respond.

Suddenly mankind never develops aeroplanes, and we're still travelling in boats or horse-drawn carriages.

You can fly.

We all can.

I travel a lot (as of very early 2020 permanently) and am constantly flying from one country to another.

### *Reason 2: You Believe Only Children Can Get Good at Languages*

I once taught private lessons to a Japanese guy in his 90s. He learned *fast*. His mind was as sharp as a razor, and he had energy that would put a 20-year-old to shame. He had a wicked sense of humour too – his jokes were dirty and made even me blush (and trust me, that's hard to do).

On the other hand, I know someone who is a great person, but severely limits herself with some rather bizarre beliefs about language learning.

She believes only kids can get good at languages and therefore it's impossible for her to get good at Japanese (she's from the UK). She started, found it difficult, then blamed the fact she's already an adult.

*"It's not my fault,"* she said. *"I'm just too old. If only I'd been exposed to Japanese as a kid!"*

This kind of thinking is stupid… and dangerous. It's what Malcolm Gladwell refers to as a 'self-fulfilling prophesy' – you believe you can't, so you don't try. Then, because you didn't do what you wanted, you tell yourself you were right and that you couldn't – when actually you just had a stupid idea in your head and let it hold you back instead of trying.

Yes, I know this sounds crazy.

But people do stuff like this all the time.

I started learning Japanese when I was 24, and by 26, I spoke it damn well. Personally, I didn't get the memo that only kids can learn languages, so I never let it hold me back.

### Reason 3: You Believe You Have to Go to an English-Speaking Country

*"I've lived in the UK 11 years, but my English just won't improve!"* That's what Penny, one of my clients, said to me several years ago during our very first coaching session. She'd lived in the UK for 11 years, and her husband is British. She said she could understand her family in English fine, but at work things were really hard. She couldn't join conversations with co-workers and didn't understand the jokes they made. To make it worse, people wouldn't understand what she was saying. People kept asking: *"Could you say that again?"* and she felt her face going bright red every time.

Penny said her pronunciation was bad, that she made mistakes in English and that what she did say never sounded natural. She ended up feeling embarrassed every time she opened her mouth. In a nutshell, her work life had become torture for her.

When she told me this, I asked her what she was doing to improve her English. The answer was shocking, but surprisingly very, very common.

<u>*Nothing*</u>.

Like many people, Penny believed that just being in an English-speaking environment would be enough to get her good at the language. Indeed, that is *why* she went to the UK – to just "pick up" English in a "natural" environment without having to study.

Big, big mistake.

I've surveyed, interviewed and worked with thousands of people over the years, and something which comes up again and again is that people hold themselves back with false beliefs about what's called "natural" learning.

There has been a ton of research done on "natural" learning methods that claim you can learn through lots of listening and just being in an English environment. *The results are not great*.

In his book, *"A Cognitive Approach to Language Learning,"* Peter Skehan talks about what's called "immersion" schooling, and how students generally become very good at listening to English...but *not* very good at speaking.

The belief that being in an English-speaking environment, or that you can learn just by listening, persists because people *want* to believe it – not because it's actually true. Many people like Penny go to live in an English-speaking country and expect that to be enough. They believe they can improve by doing nothing. So they get nothing.

One of my recent group-coaching clients was telling us how he lived in the UK for five years, but didn't improve at all. He didn't start to improve until he started thinking about what he really wanted, and consciously and actively started to apply what he'd learned from me. Hanako, another coaching client, lived in the US for 17 years and said basically the same thing. It's a very, very common experience.

Simply put, living in an English speaking country will give you more opportunities to do stuff in English – but that's it. Nothing more. By itself, just living there is not sufficient.

Being exposed to more English will help to keep your level where it is... but without the right kind of learning routine (we'll talk about this in Chapter 4), your English won't grow, and you'll keep repeating the same mistakes again and again, creating bad habits and generally making your English worse, not better.

### Reason 4: You Believe You Can Listen Your Way to Fluency

The human brain is fucking lazy.

Really, really, *really* fucking lazy.

This is for a very good reason. Energy and computational power are both limited resources… and so the more the brain can save, the better.

For the most part, this is a very, very good thing. Scientists estimate the brain processes around 11 million bits of information per second – but the conscious mind can only process around 200. Working memory—like your brain's RAM—can only hold between 4 and 7 items at a time.

If your idea of learning is just passively watching crap on YouTube, watching TV or listening to the radio without paying much attention to the language… well, your brain is going to assume it's not important.

Now, don't get me wrong. This kind of exposure to English is helpful: but only when combined with the correct focused study and learning.

When it comes to growing and improving your English, the more you can do to make your brain work, the better. So, for example, watching a film in English without subtitles is much better than watching a film with subtitles in your native language (which is a total waste of time for learning). In the same way, developing listening skills using exercises and techniques such as 'Dictation' (more on this in Chapter 11) that forces you to focus and be *active* will be much, much better than just watching a film or listening to a podcast.

I'll talk about the benefits of "dictation' later in this book, but for now, let me give you another example just to really drive home the point...

Have you ever done any kind of muscle training?

Building muscle and improving fluency in a language is very, very similar. You do an exercise that's designed to stimulate your muscle and make it grow. Now, I'm not that strong, and I'm a total beginner. So for something like a bench press, I only need about 40 kg. My personal trainer, on the other hand, who has been doing it for years and is MASSIVE, needs 200 kg or more.

You build muscle by forcing it to work beyond its current ability. You're literally tearing the muscle so that it will grow back bigger and stronger.

Now imagine my PT doing bench presses with my 40 kg. How much do you think that is going to help him build muscle?

Nothing.

My weights are far, far too light for him.

I'm a beginner – he is advanced.

This is exactly the same for your English – as a beginner you probably improved quite fast, because *everything* was difficult and intense. Just trying to understand a film in English was a very hard, active process. But the better you get, the more intensity you need to keep improving and growing.

For you, at your level, passively watching videos on YouTube or listening to English is like my PT lifting my tiny little weights.

When you study and practise English, you should feel like someone who has just lifted 200 kg – absolutely exhausted.

### Reason 5: You Don't Have Native Speakers to "Practise" with… and You Think That's a Problem

In 2009, the English learning industry in Japan was estimated to generate 670 billion yen yearly – that's about six billion dollars.

English education is one of Japan's most profitable industries. But how many people in Japan speak English at a level that matches their investment?

Almost none.

Sure, there are some people who are good at English.

A few are *really* good.

But they are exceptional people – and there certainly aren't as many of them as there are people spending money on English.

Right away this suggests that if you want to become an *extraordinary* speaker, it's not enough to study English in the same way as everybody else. You've got to do what the exceptional people do.

The way most English schools teach English really isn't that good. You see, the schools are far more interested in making a profit than they are in good teaching. And you can't really blame them – they are businesses first and foremost.

They tell you things like: *"You learned grammar in school… now to get fluent, all you need to do is practise with a native speaker!"*

It sounds great, and people buy into it.

But if you think about it, why do these schools advocate this method? It's not because it's effective; it's because it allows them to hire unqualified teachers who just chat to people for low pay.

Yes, chatting with native speakers will help with your fluency in some ways – it is something you do in English, after all. But it's not very effective, and what helps you improve is nothing to do with the fact you're speaking to a native speaker. Not only this, but my own (published) research shows very, very clearly that in Japan at least – people did NOT learn the English they need at school.

The English they're taught in school is weird as hell and has very little to no real-world utility. I'll talk more about this (and the danger of using bad materials) later in this book.

We'll also talk about what really *is* important for building fluency later, in Chapter 10.

### *Reason 6: You Need to Be Perfect before You Start Doing Anything*

This is a question I got in my email a few years ago from somebody:

*"Will I ever manage to be fluent enough to move from France to a new job in the United Kingdom?"*

Sadly, the answer to this question is *no*.

Not because it's not possible. But because we human beings are never perfectly prepared for *anything*. Good enough is good enough. You've got to just do it, and worry about the details later.

A good—and very honest—analogy for this is having children.

My first son was born in 2008. Even the mathematically challenged will quickly see that I must have been pretty damn young when he was born. I was 24, actually. Twenty-three when my girlfriend got pregnant. We weren't that careful, and before we knew it we had a choice to make: have the baby or get an abortion.

I'm not against abortion, but I'm also not deluded into thinking the time has to be "right." We both wanted kids anyway, so it was an easy choice for us to make. If everybody waited until conditions were perfect before having kids, the human race would be long extinct. There is always some reason to wait until later.

Were there times when I felt jealous of my friends out drinking and partying while I was stuck at home changing dirty nappies?

Sure.

Does it matter?

No.

And does it mean everything will always work out perfectly?

No.

Ultimately, my marriage didn't work out, and we separated. But that doesn't mean it wasn't a valuable and incredibly fulfilling experience. It's the same with English.

You can always learn a little more, get a little better. But what this means is there's no point in waiting. And anyway; the most powerful learning experiences come from doing real things in the real world with your English. So waiting to be "ready" is not only impossible, it's also a bad way to approach mastering English.

Perhaps you want to work in an international company, or you want to live and work overseas – now is the time to do it.

No matter how crap you think your English is, it doesn't matter. JFDI.


### *Reason 7: You Believe You Don't Have Time*

*"I don't have time to improve my English!"*, many people cry!

Bullshit.

Trust me, you have time.

There is not one of us in this world who has less time than we need. Ultimately, every one of us has 24 hours in a day, which is 1,440 minutes, or 86,400 seconds. And in that time most of us do very little, while a few people get incredible amounts of stuff done.

Time is never the problem. It's always about how you use your time. One of my clients said he didn't join my coaching course for several months because he knew he wouldn't have time. He was too busy with his job. But here's the thing – his job was all in English. He was always busy because he was constantly fighting fires. Nothing got done ahead of time, and he was always panicking to finish things last minute.

Then one day he realised that he wasn't getting anything done because his bad English kept slowing him down. Reading, writing and replying emails took far, far too long. He'd misunderstand something in a meeting and waste time trying to fix it later. He'd struggle to communicate things to others – which would waste even more time.

Clearly then, the best thing for him to do was to stop everything and improve his English first.

### Reason 8: Your Thinking is too Simplistic

This is related to some of the previous points, but I'm including it as its own separate point because it's important. Simplistic thinking. People tend to think they can "just" do one simple thing and they'll master English – you can't.

One of my most popular YouTube videos is the "Shadowing" exercise video.

And I'm forever getting comments and emails from people saying things like, *"I do your shadowing method but I'm not improving"*.

What else are they doing?

Nothing.

First, Shadowing isn't a method – it's just one exercise among many I use with my clients. Second, it has to be used as a larger English workout routine. Third, it's only useful if your problem can be fixed by shadowing.

(I've got a free 5-step guide called "The Good Shadowing Guide" here: https://doingenglish.com/ shadowing if you want to learn when—and when not —to use Shadowing, as well as exactly how to do it correctly).

The same is true of "I just need to learn more words" – that's not true. It's also the same for "I just need to learn more grammar!". "If I just lived in an English speaking country", is another one, that we've already discussed.

Look: language is complex.

And that means there are many areas you have to develop – just learning more words will do nothing for your fluency and studying more grammar will do nothing for your naturalness.

Throughout this book, I'm going to demonstrate that simply learning more, more, MORE words will do nothing for your fluency. I'm also going to demonstrate why studying grammar rules is not only not helping you to sound more accurate and natural, it's actually making your problem worse.

### Reason 9: You're all study all the time

So far in many the points above, I've talked about the importance of study and putting focused time and effort into improving and growing your English. But if you're studying all the time, you'll also have other big problems.

There's a saying in English: *"All work and no play makes jack a dull boy"*. Well, as far as improving your English speaking is concerned, this is also very, very true.

Later in this book we'll talk extensively about the "Two Track Approach" and how it helps to solve what I call "English Learner Imbalance". In a nutshell, if you're all study, all the time and **ALWAYS** trying to learn and improve in English, then that's all you'll get good at – being an English *learner*. But you don't want to be an English *learner* – you want to be an English *speaker*.

So for example, you might watch a film in English. But you're not actually watching it. You're trying to catch words and constantly pausing, writing things down in your notebook or looking things up in the dictionary. Suddenly, what should be a fun pleasurable activity becomes a learning exercise. And this tells your brain *English is different to my native language – we study and analyse it, not use it.*

Again, you get good at what you do. And so you'll only ever get good at being an English learner and suffer from very real speaking problems; real people in real conversation don't have pause buttons, after all. You can't stop and look things up. You can't slow them down. So you become overwhelmed and can't keep up.

This is what happens when you're all study all the time, but there's also a film side. People who are all 'doing', and no study.

### *Reason 10: You do-do-do, but never study*

The opposite of the previous problem is people who go completely the other way. They never study.

They only ever chat and watch films, listen to podcasts and feel like they're doing something useful to improve their English… but in reality, they're not really doing anything at all.

There's a ton of research that shows just exposing yourself to English is very ineffective for learning it. That's why just living in an English speaking country isn't enough. It's why just listen, listen, listen! doesn't work. You will pick words and bits of English up, yes. But it won't be consistent. And it will be slow.

If you remember the example of Penny I talked about above, this is what she—and many people going to live in English-speaking countries—did. She thought just being there was enough. But really, being there just keeps what you've got, and never adds anything new to it. You simply keep recycling the same English, making the same mistakes and saying the same things again. And you end up creating bad habits that are hard to fix.

To really improve, you need a balance of <u>both</u> focused learning—where the goal is to grow your English— and of 'doing' in the same way as you do things in your native language – where the goal is to train your mind to use English subconsciously, just like your native language.

I call this the 'Two-Track Approach', and we'll talk more about it in Chapter 4.

Before we get to that, though, we need to take a step back and think about <u>WHY</u> you are here.

## CHAPTER 2
## START WITH WHY

ACCORDING TO LINGUIST DAVID CRYSTAL, around 1 billion people speak English, and about 2/3 of these speak English as a second language. That's right – far more people speak English as a second language than as a first language.

This makes English a damn useful language to master. In fact, these days English is pretty much essential for international business. Will that change in the future? Maybe, but not any time soon.

This does, however, also mean you've got a lot of competition.

Speaking Japanese at a high level is a huge advantage for me simply because very few people can do it (even among people living in Japan). When I worked as a Japanese—English translator (for a very, very short amount of time) it was easy to get jobs simply because there was almost no competition.

Not so with English.

English is a bit like getting a PhD. It's a very difficult thing to do, and it looks big and impressive to people who are not part of the world of academia.

However, the reality is that if you want an academic career, getting the PhD is simply the first step. It's the key which opens the door… but once you've opened the door, you're just one among many other people who have the same key as you. In academia *everybody* has a PhD – so it's no advantage at all.

Same with English skills.

Just getting good at English may open some doors for you, but it's not enough to give you a real advantage.

For that… you have to be *extraordinary*.

One of my coaching clients, Bobby, told me he was struggling to stand out in his workplace. He was part of the sales team in a Hong Kong-based tech company, and most deals were made with overseas companies. Bobby spoke English well – but no matter how hard he tried, he was always pushed back into the shadows by another sales rep who spoke much, much better

English. Bobby told me about a time when he met a group of Japanese clients at the airport, and one of them said to the super-star English speaker, *"Your English is so good! I thought you were born in an English-speaking country!"*

Every time Bobby spoke, the clients would speak to his colleague instead. Whenever the clients had a question, they asked the colleague – even when Bobby was the expert in that area.

I'm sure you can imagine how frustrating this was. But the truth was, Bobby was only *okay* at English – and his colleague was better.

Another coaching client, Hanako, told me about a friend who always seemed to be ahead of her. They both went to live in the US at the same time, and both started working at the same place. But the friend was much better at English and was quickly promoted from an assistant position to a full position. Then, after just two years, she was promoted again to a job with more responsibility and a higher salary. Hanako, however, lagged behind, always in her friend's shadow.

## It's Dog-Eat-Dog out There

Of the billion people in the world who speak English, some of them will be your friends, colleagues and clients – people who help you in life. But the vast majority will be your competitors.

It's a dog-eat-dog world out there.

You are swimming in a sea of competition and just having English is not enough anymore. Ultimately, the person who speaks best *wins*. And I want you to be that person.

So how do you become the person who speaks best? First and foremost, you need to be clear about your "Why?" What is it that you want to achieve in English? Nobody wants to get good at English just for the hell of it. We all have a need deep down: we want to be respected in our workplace or by our friends and family. We want to make more money and live easier. Or we simply want to make it through the day without feeling embarrassed in front of our co-workers. Regardless, it all starts here with your *Why.*

Imagine this situation: two rowing teams are racing to London.

The first team consists of two normal guys in the oldest, worst piece of junk you can imagine. Their boat is falling to bits. There are holes in it. Water is coming in. They're paddling down the River Thames at just 10 feet a day.

Then you have their competition: they're Olympic rowers. They're in a state-of-the-art kayak and they've got super expensive equipment.

Who is going to get to London first?

You might think it would be the Olympians, because they're the ones with speed, strength and the best equipment. But what I didn't tell you is this: *They are paddling up the river, going the wrong way.* They're paddling like crazy, going full force from morning until night. But they never stopped to ask themselves: *"Are we going in the right direction?"*

It sounds so obvious.

But I see English learners do this all the time. They say they want to get fluent. They want to be like a 'native speaker'. But they've never stopped to ask themselves, *"Is what I'm doing now taking me in the right direction?"*

If it's not, it's a waste of time.

Many people are reading the newspaper, looking words up in the dictionary and expecting to magically get better in conversation. But news English and conversational English is totally different. Out of the 500 most frequent chunks—more on *chunks* later—in both conversation and news-English, only 20 chunks match. Four-hundred and eighty are totally different. This tells you that learning newspaper English is useless for conversation.

That's a simple example, and there are many, many others. I already mentioned in the previous chapter how people use exercises like 'shadowing' to improve, but never ask themselves if it's the right exercise for them.

With everything you do, you've got to be moving in the right direction, not away from your goals. Because, if you're at least going in the right direction, you'll get there eventually, even if what you're doing isn't perfect.

For my PhD research, I did a series of research projects in Japanese secondary schools. First, I analysed the textbooks and teaching materials they use, then I tested them in a laboratory to see how fluent the students were in the English they'd been taught.

Guess what?

They were very fluent: the students had successfully acquired all the language in their textbooks, and they processed it just like a native speaker would – automatically and without consciously thinking about it. But here's the thing: the language in their textbooks is totally different to the language people actually use in the real world, just like newspaper-English is different to conversational English. So although these students were getting fluent… they were getting fluent in something totally useless.

Other people are spending all their time studying more English, when the truth is their English is already good enough – they just haven't developed confidence in using it, so they constantly doubt themselves.

Others think people avoid them because they make grammar mistakes… when in reality, it's their personality people avoid. Harsh, yes, but better to know than not.

### *Why Are You Here?*

In his book and TED talks presentation, Simon Sinek urges business owners to *start with why*.

*"People don't buy what you do, they buy why you do it,"* he says.

Sinek gives the example of Apple computer – why are they consistently more innovative and more successful than their competitors? After all, Apple is just a computer company. But other computer manufacturers are busy trying to tell you what they do (make computers) and how they do it (it's got lots of RAM and a big hard drive), and that is boring and uninspiring.

Apple, on the other hand, tells you *why* they do what they do: Apple wants to challenge the status quo and change the world through better design. Apple aims to change people's lives; they just happen to do this by making computers.

Incidentally, I'm an Apple user, and the thought of buying (or even using) a Windows computer makes me sick. You could say I am well and truly sold on Apple's "Why".

Now, you'd do well to take Sinek's advice when thinking about your own work and business, but also know this: *exactly the same is true of your English, too.*

This book is written for people who need English in their business, work and lives. Whatever it is you do, you need to get clear on *why* you do it. English itself is just a tool, you see. Something you use in your life to achieve your goals. English is not your *Why*. English is the *How* of the *Why* – or, to put it another way, it's the tool you'll use to achieve those dreams, but not the dream itself. So your first step should be to answer the question: "What do you want *to do* with English?"

I work with a wide range of people including artists, photographers, IT professionals, doctors, teachers, fashion designers, marketing consultants, salesmen and business owners, business executives, directors and non-native English teachers. All of them are people who have already reached a fairly high level of English, but they suffer from the same problem: *their English holds them back and stops them from being what they could —and* should *—be*. Their business suffers because of their English, and inside, they suffer too. In a nutshell, they are people who are painfully aware of the fact they're speaking in a second language.

It's easy to get stuck and overwhelmed at this stage. After all, there is so much English out there to learn. How do you cut through it all? How do you figure out what you need to do?

It all starts with your *Why*.

One of my coaching clients told me she was worried about joining a big conference at her company. She didn't think her English was good enough for it. With a little help from me (and a lot of hard work on her part), she performed brilliantly, moved to a different position (for considerably more money) and then started her own business. She was able to do this because she was very clear about what she wanted to achieve with her English.

Another of my clients—a freelance artist—was literally told to, *"Go away and come back when you can speak English!"* by an editor at an art conference. She had travelled halfway around the world just to meet that editor. Of course this was very painful, but it also gave her the motivation to work hard on improving her English. And she has a clear goal that she wants to achieve: her *Why* is taking her artwork out into the world and proving that cunt of an editor wrong – will he regret rejecting her because of her English? *You damn bet your life he will!*

Yet another client needed to teach physics classes at his school in English. The first time he taught a class, his students laughed at him because of his accent and because they were better at English than him. For him, his *Why* was becoming the leader he needed to be for his students.

Another student of mine found himself in a similar position in his company – he was a senior level executive, and he needed to be a strong leader. But he felt

embarrassed speaking English around his subordi-
nates, because they were much better at English. Same
*Why*, different situation.

*My goal is to help you forget that English isn't your first
language* so you can get on with doing whatever it is
you do best, without English getting in the way. But I
can only do that if you are clear about your *Why*. All
the situations I described above come with very
powerful emotions – it's not just about getting fluent
in English, it's about doing things in English and how
you *feel* when you do them.

### Here's What I Want You to Do…

Get a piece of paper and write out a minimum of 50
things you want to achieve in your work, and a
minimum of 50 things you want to do in your
personal life.

Not things like "speak fluent English"—remember;
that's *how* you do something, not *why* you do it—but
actual things you want to achieve.

It might be visiting a certain country. Personally I love
running, and I want to run a marathon on all seven
continents. It might be starting your own business. Or
getting a job at a certain company.

Don't overthink it: just write out two long lists.

Then, look at each one and ask yourself how English can help you achieve those goals. Remember: English is <u>how</u> you do it, not *why*. English is only for doing better things; it's not the thing you do itself.

You'll also need to be honest about what English will do for you. Many people will start by saying empty things like, "Because English is a global language" – but is that really your *Why?* Unlikely.

The truth is, you could travel in a foreign country without knowing English. I recently spent a month in Taiwan without speaking a word of Chinese beyond a few basic phrases. It's amazing how much you can get done by pointing or using your phone. But I wish I'd learned more Chinese – it would have made the experience a lot more fun and removed some of the frustration. It would also have been a great boost for my ego. Simply put, it would have been fun and I would have felt good seeing people impressed by my Chinese speaking. Respect from others is a powerful motivator, after all.

In fact, for many people speaking better English may be more about status or even wanting to be better at something than your friends than anything else. It might also be about getting work done faster, with less hassle or it might be about proving to someone that you can do it. It might be about meeting people, making friends or even finding a boyfriend or girlfriend.

These are all good reasons.

Think of a guy going to the gym and working out every day. Why is he doing it? Is it because he wants to look amazing on the beach and sleep with girls, or is it because he's so overweight and unhealthy he could die if he doesn't? Or a woman whose husband left her for someone younger and more attractive – is she going to the gym to feel more healthy, or does she want to get in shape to make her ex-husband regret leaving her? In both cases, the "how" is the same – but the *why* is very different. Some *Whys* are practical; others are emotional.

You just need to be clear on what you'll do with English, and what exactly is important to you about speaking English well in that situation.

### A Final Note on Goals

Earl Nightingale says there are two kinds of people: goal-driven people and what he calls "river people."

Goal-driven people are driven by big, impressive goals – things that might take a lifetime to achieve. River people, on the other hand, have no big goal: they are just hopping from one rock to the next in the great river of life.

I'm a river person.

I have many small goals... but no single "big" goal. I like to do things in a very flexible way, and I change direction fast and often. Now, you're probably thinking that this completely contradicts everything I said above. But what you have to understand is that your *Why* and your "goals" are not necessarily the same thing.

You see, being a "river" person doesn't mean that you work randomly. Just this morning I was talking with a new client. She's at around the low-intermediate level and wants to get better at speaking English. She's clever and motivated, so she'll do fine. But the first thing I noticed is that her *Why* was rather vague – especially concerning English. She had goals and things she wanted to do, but she wasn't really very clear on them, or why English would be important for her.

This is a problem, because the brain needs context in order to remember the language you use.

When you hear new phrases and expressions, you need to connect them to a situation, otherwise they'll just be forgotten. For example, say you dream of becoming a professional photographer, and you have a clear goal of taking photographs and displaying them in exhibitions all over the world, speaking in English with gallery owners and art-lovers. Well, suddenly all the English you learn has far more meaning, because you have a clear vision of the situations in which you want to use it. You hear someone say something like, "Good afternoon!" and you imagine yourself *right there*, at that exhibition, saying "Good afternoon!" to someone who's just walked through the door.

This is very, very powerful.

And combined with the motivation that comes from being clear about your deeper emotional drive—more money? Freedom from embarrassment? Status? Perhaps even sex?—if you're clear about this stuff, you'll be unstoppable.

We're going to talk more about learning the language itself later, but understand right here, right now, that the stronger your *Why*, the faster you will improve. It will guide you, focus you, and give you something very concrete to work towards.

Think long and hard about the things you want to do in life. Your goals might change (mine often do), and that's fine. What's important is that you can imagine yourself doing things in English and you can *feel* the way you want to feel when you speak.

**CHAPTER 3**
**LEARNING ENGLISH 101**

WHEN I DID my master's degree, I'd been struggling with Japanese for a long time. But very quickly I realised the reason I had been struggling was because I was *thinking* about language in totally the wrong way.

Remember what I said in the Chapter 1?

Your mindset is everything.

If the way you think about English and English learning is wrong, you will take the wrong actions, and in turn get the wrong results.

### What Even Is Language?

You'd think this would be an easy question to answer. But it's not – far from it. And for me, at least, the definition of *language* provided by language scientists (also sometimes called "psycholinguists") is unsatisfactory. So, after giving you this definition, I'll give you my own.

My definition of language might sound a bit *weird*. I was an artist long before I got into the world of second-language acquisition, and I primarily think in metaphors. And that's exactly what the definition I will give you is – a metaphor.

But first, here's the official definition. In the 1960s, Charles F. Hockett came up with a set of features that characterise human language. We say "human language", because although animals do have language, it's clearly not the same as human language. Animals can speak (some better than others) but none can do what humans can do. Indeed, our ability to use language is what separates us as a species.

Originally, Hockett's list had 13 features, but arguably some aren't necessary for language. Speaking and listening are a great example – sign language does a pretty good job of being "language" without speaking or listening. So clearly they aren't necessary. Here I'm just including the features that are necessary.

First, a language must communicate meaning. Often that is by speaking and writing, but it doesn't have to be – I can communicate "hello" with a smile and a wave just as easily as I can by saying the word, for example.

Second, the language itself is arbitrary. What we mean by this is the words themselves are just symbols. The words "rock" and "ishi" (Japanese) both stand for the same thing – it's just that the word is different. But neither word is better than the other. The word "rock" isn't more descriptive than "ishi". They're just different. And totally arbitrary. We could choose to call a rock a "bligbopper" if we wanted, and it would be just as good.

The sounds of language must fit into distinct categories, or, to put it simply, a language has a limited number of sounds. The number is different between languages: English has about 40 phonemes (basic sounds), Japanese has about 46, some languages have a lot more, some a lot less. But the number of sounds we produce has to be limited.

Language must be able to communicate events which are happening away from the speaker in terms of time and location. This is one of the main things that separates us from other animals. Monkeys, for example, communicate information about predators using distinct sounds. But they only do it when the predator is *present* – they can't talk about a predator that was there, or one that a friend saw. Humans can.

Finally, languages are "generative" in that a limited number of units, whether words, rules, chunks, phrases or expressions, can be used to create an infinite number of sentences.

Now, this is a start.

It does a great job of describing the features of language. But if you ask me, it doesn't get to the *heart* of the question. While it's great to know what the features are, just like it's helpful to know roses are red and grass is green (unless you're colour blind like my friend Kevin…), I still don't really know *what* language is. And herein lies my criticism of academia.

Science has to be exact, precise and objective. But by doing so, it often sacrifices usefulness.

Everything in this book is based on hard science and research, some of which has been done and published by me. Much from my reading of academic literature. But it's also based on experience teaching and learning – and that, often, is far more useful than what science can tell us. I mention this right here, right now, because a lot of people will tell you that their methods are "based on science" – but really, what does that mean? Even if this is true, it may not be very helpful to you. Being "based on science" doesn't make it helpful, after all, or even mean that it works.

So let me give you my personal definition of what language is. As I warned you before, it's a little weird. But bear with me.

## *"The Beast"*

One of my favourite places in the world is Shinjuku Station. It is certainly not the biggest station in the world, but it is the busiest. In 2007, it was estimated that each and every day more than 4 million people pass through the train station. That number certainly hasn't gone down over the years.

The reason it is so busy is it acts as the hub station for everyone coming in and out of Tokyo, as well as for a lot of people going around Tokyo. But Shinjuku Station is not simply a building in the middle of the city.

It's alive – a gigantic beast that heaves, groans and pulsates with the flow of human traffic. A massive heart that keeps people flowing around the city like blood through veins. Put simply, it's people who give Shinjuku Station life.

No one comes to the station because they love the station. The destination is never the station. It's never about wanting to use the station to get somewhere. *It's all about the destination.*

People pass through the station because it's the fastest, most efficient way to get to where they want to go. So in many ways it's similar to language.

The actual words and grammar are meaningless. What matters is the *destination* – whether what you're doing gets you to the place you want to go.

We use language to exchange information, bond socially, express emotion, play, and even organise our thoughts. But it goes deeper than that, much deeper. We need to think about why we even have language in the first place. If I ask you, *"What is a pen?"* you'd probably tell me that it's a tool for writing. And therein lies the problem – language is a tool, but unlike a pen, it's quite hard to define what we actually do with it.

Go back to the image of a train station.

People channelled, streaming through tunnels en route to their destination. Like electricity running through the power grid, water through pipes. A giant network. That network is humanity. *Life.* An entity

that is at once a single, living being and simultane-
ously a collection of smaller parts.

You are a part of that network.

We're all born with a cable and a plug that connects
directly to a socket in that human network.

Go ahead. Plug it in.

Congratulations!

You've just connected with the rest of the human race.
Language is that cable. It's a 255 terabits per second
fibre-optic super-cable, capable of transmitting the
entire human experience from person to person in the
blink of an eye.

Emotion. Information. Pain. Sorrow. Love. Hate. Indif-
ference. Recognition. Denial. Education and
ignorance.

Language has the power to teach, the power to
confuse and the power to overwhelm.

If you don't believe me, think back to the first time the
love of your life whispered *'I love you'* in your ear and
the time she told you, *'It's over… I met someone else'*.

People are so concerned with words, grammar,
phrasal verbs and idioms. But these things are mean-

ingless by themselves. Those things are just components of the cable – the raw materials it's made from. But they are not the reason you need the cable, neither are they the cable itself.

You will realise I'm talking in metaphors here. But in my experience the biggest breakthroughs come from understanding this simple point – speaking English is not a goal, *it's a tool you can use to achieve a goal.*

You need a *Why*—a goal—that is greater than English itself. So if you didn't take the time to get clear on your *Why*, stop here, and go back to the previous chapter.

### What Is Language Learning?

You probably studied English at school. Or at least something that resembles English (remember what I said in Chapter 2 about the research I did on secondary school English – yes, it was made of English words, but no, it wasn't anything like actual English).

If the English classes you had at school were anything like the way I studied French, you were taught English as an *academic* subject. By "academic" subject, I mean something that you studied in much the same way as mathematics, science or history. Memorising facts, random words, random grammar points. And then we're expected to perform well on tests.

Unfortunately, though, this is a pretty crap way to go about learning a language.

And in fact, in many cases it's damaging.

It promotes a slow, conscious form of speaking using words and grammar rules and focusing on accuracy. Your teacher punished you for mistakes—many of which weren't actually mistakes; they were just different to what your teacher wanted—but never rewarded you for speaking fluently, without hesitation.

You also had subjects like sport, music and art.

Well, guess what?

English is like sport, music and art – but *not* like math or history. It's something that you have to do and experience and feel – not just with your mind, but with your physical body.

Have you ever sailed a yacht before?

I haven't.

But it wouldn't matter how many books I read about sailing – if I got on a yacht now and took it out to sea I would die. No two ways about it. *I'd sink the damn thing and drown.* If you were stupid enough to get in the yacht with me, you'd die too.

See, I have no idea how to sail. And theory is not enough. Yes, you do have to learn it, just like you have to learn English. Knowing that the yacht moves forward when wind blows into its sails is essential information, but this isn't going to help me much when I'm racing full speed towards a cliff. It's something that you have to do and experience to get good at bit at a time.

The key to getting better at speaking a language, then, is *experience*. The more you do, the better you get. Learn, do, repeat.

Experience drives learning.

I suggest you write that down and stick it to your computer monitor or something. Perhaps tattoo it on your forehead so you see it every time you look in the mirror.

It's the things that we do in the language that promote acquisition of the language. It's what we *do* that makes us learn and get good at the language.

On the surface, this seems simple – experience drives learning. But as is often the case, the devil is in the details.

You see, experience is experience.

There is no real difference between positive experiences and negative experiences. They both provide feedback and learning opportunities to some degree. Normally, though, a *negative* experience is a far more powerful learning opportunity simply because the fact that you've screwed up means there's something to learn from.

Also, "experience" with language <u>does not</u> mean only speaking. Speaking is simply one part of English. The deepest kind of learning comes not from just speaking, or just listening, but from understanding the language-learning process *holistic*ally.

### Holistic Learning

One of the best films I've seen in the last few years is *"Slumdog Millionaire"* from 2008. Visually, the film is absolutely stunning. If you're into cinematography like I am, definitely watch it.

The story follows 18-year-old Jamal Malik, an Indian Muslim from the slum. He ends up on the game show

"Who wants to be a millionaire?", and at the beginning the host laughs at him. *A boy from the slum? He doesn't stand a chance!* But Malik knows the answers to all the questions… and as he progresses, the host gets more and more worried that he might actually win.

The show ends before the final question, and the host has Malik arrested – he must be cheating, he thinks. So Jamal Malik ends up in a prison cell, being interrogated by the police. How did he cheat? Where did he get the answers from? Again, the assumption is that a kid from the slum who's never been to school could never get the answers right.

It all turns out to be pure luck, though. Malik had a hard life, and experienced many things – some good, but most terrible. For example, one question he was asked was: "In depictions of God Rama, he is famously holding what in his right hand?"

All of a sudden, Malik remembers his childhood. Some Hindus attacked the slum and killed his mother. Malik and his brother ran away… and as they did, they encountered a Hindu child dressed as the God Rama. The image is burned into his memory like a photograph – a child painted blue, left hand held in the air, and the right hand clutching a bow and arrow. How could Malik *not* get the question right?

The film progresses, and by pure chance each question corresponds with an experience Malik had in his life. So although he didn't go to school, had no education and never studied… he knew all the answers.

Obviously, this is a story, but it perfectly demonstrates the concept of holistic learning. It's learning from experience in the real world and putting together all the knowledge you have to form a strong *whole*. (The adjective 'holistic' comes from the word 'whole' – even though you can't see it from the way they're spelt.)

Think of a car.

Viewed in one way, a car is also a pile of car parts. Really, the pile of car parts and the car are the same thing. Physically, at least, there is no difference between them. But obviously the parts scattered all over the floor and the assembled car are not the same thing.

Knowledge is the same. It's learned in parts, but becomes something totally different when it is assembled. Holistic learning looks at the car – not the parts. It looks at the whole, not the individual components.

Your learning time is when you collect the parts, but you've also got to put them together via your real-world experience in English.

In a moment we'll talk about the three things you need to speak English well – something I call the "LKC Triangle", and you will see that language is only one component of the car. You also need other things to speak English well.

Language is far, far more than a set of words, phrases and grammar patterns. Those things are only components of the car – just like we talked about above, when I discussed the question "What is language?" You need to look beyond that. Focus not on the car parts, but on the *whole car* when it's assembled properly and ready to go somewhere.

Only when you start to do this does the next question become obvious: *What kind of car do you want?*

Do you want a flashy sports car, a classic, something practical? Perhaps you want a Rolls Royce? How about a Jaguar?

Each of these is a type of car. But there's a massive difference between a Ferrari and my dad's battered old Ford.

You see, depending on what you want to do with your English—your *Why*—the dream "car" that *you* want is going to be quite different to the car someone else wants. And so are the parts that go into it. Do you see now why I was so insistent on your thinking about your *Why*? The things you want to do? The things you want to achieve in life?

Your *Why* might change over time – just like someone might decide to trade in their Ferrari in favour of a Jaguar – and some days you'll need a different type of English to others (just like you might drive your Ford to the supermarket, but the Benz to a fancy party).

Good communication comes from thinking about English holistically – as a whole.

Most people spend far, far too much time worrying about insignificant things like whether they picked the right word or whether a certain phrase is better than another. Yes, those things are important. But they're only a single part of the equation.

### *The Three Things You Need to Speak English Well*

In order to speak a language really well, you need three things. I call this the "LKC Triangle".

You need the L, which is *Language.*

This much is obvious: if you don't have the words and phrases that you need to express the things you want to say, clearly you're not going to be able to say them.

But although learning the language itself is important, by itself language isn't enough.

You also need the "K" of the LKC Triangle – *Knowledge*.

If you have no knowledge or understanding of a given topic, you're not going to be able to talk about it well (or even at all). If you asked me to talk about electrical engineering, I wouldn't be able to. I haven't got a clue about electrical engineering. I'm not even completely sure what electrical engineering is, other than that it's related to electricity… and probably engineering. I couldn't talk about it in English, Japanese, or Chinese; I couldn't talk about it in *any* language. Even a language I know really well. Because I don't have the background knowledge.

There's one more thing you need. C for *Culture.*

This is easily the most complicated part of the LKC Triangle, and the most difficult to do well. Put simply, culture is like a pair of glasses that we see the world through.

Put on a pair of pink-tinted glasses, and you'll see the world in pink. Change them for a blue-tinted pair, and the world looks different.

Culture is the filter through which you see everything. When you say something in English, you say it with your own cultural understanding. But what I hear and understand you to be saying may be totally different, because I understand things with *my* own cultural values. The more different our cultures are, the larger the gap will be.

We're going to talk about this in a lot of detail in this book because culture is really, really complicated. And it has many, many levels.

Humans have a culture that is distinct from other animals. If aliens ever visit us, they'll have a culture that is very different to ours too. We can also say that countries in one region of the world (for example, Asia) tend to have cultures that are relatively similar to each other when compared to some country in another region (for example, Africa).

We can also say that countries have cultures that are quite different. Even though it's true that the cultures in Japan and South Korea are similar if you compare either of them with the United States, the culture in Japan and South Korea are actually quite different compared to each other.

We can take this even further, because we can also say that cities inside one country have different cultures. The culture in Manchester is a bit different from the culture in London, which is different again to the culture in Exeter, or any other city in the United Kingdom.

We can also say that individuals have a culture as well. The way that I think is not the same as the way you think, which isn't the same as the way a third person thinks – even if we all live in the same city in the same country. We all have our own experience. And our experiences affect what we understand and the way we view the world.

Now, at this point you may be worried.

You came here thinking you had to learn English (which is enough by itself), but now I'm telling you that you've got lots of other stuff to learn, too.

Don't worry!

We'll cover all this stuff in detail, but I'll also explain how you can learn what you need as quickly and effectively as possible.

### *Pronunciation, Accent and Articulation*

What accent should you learn?

This is a tough question to answer, and a rather contentious topic. Accent is something that everybody has an opinion on...but something that very few people truly understand.

My (rather unpopular) answer to the question is: it doesn't matter. Or rather, your own accent is fine – as long as you sound clear and easy to understand.

I was once told a story about a Chinese guy living and working in Australia, who was having a rather hard time. He was a very high English level, and he'd spent a lot of time having accent and elocution training. He sounded exactly like a member of the British royalty with his crisp, Received Pronunciation accent (known as "RP" for short).

Lots of people want this.

But actually this was the source of his problem. Believe it or not, people in Australia found him really uncomfortable to talk to. Here's this Chinese guy, in Australia, speaking with a posh British accent.

It's actually a very, very good thing if you speak with your own accent. If you are Chinese and you have a Chinese accent, that identifies you as a Chinese person. It communicates a lot about who you are, where you come from, and your cultural identity and values. But if you hide that accent, you hide your identity. And other people can feel that you're not being true to yourself…and that makes them uncomfortable.

Not only that, but Received Pronunciation is an accent that isn't very common anymore, and it's associated with distinctions between the upper and lower classes. Upper Received Pronunciation is associated with the English aristocracy and schools such as Eton and Oxford. Someone who speaks this way can be perceived negatively – like someone who thinks they're better than other people.

The researcher Peter Trudgill estimated in 1974 that only 3% of people in Britain were actually RP speakers – and this percentage has likely decreased.

Yet another problem with speaking in a perfect native speaker accent is that it sets people's expectations very high. Many people find that when they first speak, people assume they are native speakers. This might seem like a good thing, but it creates a lot of pressure to speak perfectly. If I hear you speak and you sound Italian, I think, "Here's an Italian guy." If later on you make a mistake with your English, I don't think anything of it. I probably won't even notice. It's just natural. But if I thought you were a British native speaker? Well, any mistakes you make are going to *really* stand out.

To put it another way, speaking with an accent that isn't your own is like wearing a mask.

It feels like when you talk to someone wearing sunglasses. It can be uncomfortable to talk with them, because we miss the information we're used to getting by observing the speaker's eyes – a key part of their facial expression.

Of course, this doesn't mean it's necessarily bad to copy a native speaker accent. It just means that you should be yourself with it. Don't be fake.

This also doesn't mean you can ignore the way you sound. The trick is to speak with a *clear* accent and *clear* pronunciation. This really isn't anything to do with your accent, though. It's all about rhythm and how you group words together into 'chunks' of English (something we'll talk about more in Chapter 6). Whether you pronounce the basic sounds correctly, and whether you add stress where stress would be expected.

English has a specific rhythm and intonation – we speak in "chunks" of language, not in words.

English has this rhythm for a reason. Chunks are like "language-shortcut keys" in your head. They're used as complete units, with no grammar or individual words to put them together. Native speakers store these chunks in their heads as wholes. They use them as wholes. And they understand them as wholes. This makes them instantly understandable and makes communication MUCH faster and more efficient. But to benefit from this, **you** also have to use them as wholes – otherwise they stop being instantly under-standable.

If I say something like: "At the end of the day,", it's not: "At. The. End. Of. The. Day."

It's: "athuendvthdei,".

You've got to learn to chunk your speech in this kind of way. When you do that, you'll sound natural – even if you pronounce one or two of the words slightly wrong.

More on this later, in Chapter 6.

## CHAPTER 4

## HOW ENGLISH MASTERY
## REALLY WORKS

"*IT's the most simple things in life that are the most extraordinary,*" says Brazilian writer Paulo Coelho.

I agree.

Indeed, mastering a language is not complicated. On the contrary, it's very, _very_ simple.

One of the big mistakes I made when I was struggling with Japanese was always looking for a "better" way to learn, and "new" methods for improving. I would try things, but quickly doubt myself and end up thinking I needed to find a better way. I repeated this process again and again and again. I went from trying to learn by listening to Japanese all day, every day, to studying textbooks, to trying to learn by practising with native speakers, to trying to memorise lists of vocabulary.

All of these things can be useful as *part* of an improvement plan, but what I was doing had no balance. I *did* a lot of stuff… but it was all so random and messy. There was no structure or consistency to what I was doing. It was busy work, but not *smart* work.

The result?

My Japanese was also messy and random with no structure or consistency.

Improving in a second language is actually very, very simple. Not easy to do to be sure, but extremely simple.

It comes down to a very simple—but importantly, consistent—two-step process which I call the "Two-Track Approach".

In a nutshell:

Step 1: A short period of focused, intensive study of English (to grow your usable words, chunks, phrases and expressions etc.)

Step 2: Use what you've learned in the real world as much as you can to automate it.

Simple, right?

Yes, it is.

But as with anything, *the devil is in the details*. What language do you need to learn? What is the most effective way to learn the English you need? What is the most effective way to automate it? And what is the correct balance of learning and using?

Never fear.

That's what this chapter is all about.

### The "Imbalance" Problem

As an English learner, you have two goals.

You need to grow your English – i.e. increase the amount of usable words, chunks, phrases expressions you have. And second, to "automate" it meaning to make it smooth and fluent.

The problem is, these two goals need to be done in two different ways.

And they contradict each other.

Worse: studying English slows down the automation stage if done wrong.

You already read in Chapter 1 that if you are always studying English, always switched on to "learning"

English and constantly (consciously) trying to improve, you'll just create bad habits. You're telling your brain, *"English is different to my native language – it's something I have to study and analyse"*. And since we get good at what we do, all you'll ever get good at is being an English learner – not an English *speaker*.

On the other hand, just using English with no attempt to learn is a very, very slow way to grow your English.

Research shows that the fastest way to improve is to learn (i.e. study) first, then use what you learnt.

And to do this in the most effective way, my clients use the "Two-Track Approach".

As I said above, this is a balance of focused, intense learning where you spend 30 minutes to an hour every day studying and learning the English you need.

This is your growth time.

This is the time for analysing.

Trying to understand.

Looking stuff up in the dictionary.

Using practise exercises.

In a nutshell, this is your time for being an English learner.

Then, outside of that focused block of time you use English as much as you can: but <u>without</u> trying to learn.

You just treat it in the same way as your native language. You <u>do</u> English, not learn it. In other words, this is your time for being an English *speaker*.

This approach allows you to grow your English fast, while also developing the correct habits in your head by telling your brain: *"English is the same as my native language"*.

### *Focused Intensive Learning*

Right now—and I mean, *right now*—I want you to go to your calendar, and schedule between 30 minutes and an hour of time every day for English study.

Do it now.

This is your study time.

And if English is important to you, you <u>will</u> turn up each and every day to do it. Treat it as important. Treat this time in the same as you treat turning up for your job or a meeting – you wouldn't just decide not to do those things. So don't just decide not to do your English study time.

What if you think you're too busy?

You're not.

If you think creatively, you will find time.

And honestly, if you absolutely do not have 30 minutes a day to work on your English? You have **much** bigger problems in your life than English, so close this book now and go and sort those out first.

In Chapter 1 I told you about how several years ago one of my coaching clients—Takumi—worked in an international company in Japan and consistently had trouble at work because of his English. He wasted a lot of time because of misunderstandings and mistakes and ended up having to work a lot of overtime (often unpaid). Obviously, his incompetence made him very, very unpopular with his boss and co-workers, too. The solution was both simple and obvious: fix his damn English.

Now, what I didn't tell you in Chapter 1 was *how* he did it. You see, this guy was already super busy. His schedule was jam-packed, and he thought there was no way he could find time or studying English. But there was a simple solution.

Takumi travelled to work every day on one of Tokyo's high-speed commuter trains. If you've ever seen videos of rush-hour trains in Tokyo, you'll know they're unbelievably crowded. You may have even seen on TV the station employees with white gloves whose job it is to push people into the train so the doors can close. But many of these trains also often have a "green car" – which is basically a first-class carriage where it's quieter and you can sit down. And that's what Takumi did. He got himself a pass for the green car and used this time for his English every day. Forty minutes to work; forty minutes back. Suddenly he had just over an hour every day to dedicate to this English.

To make a long story short, Takumi improved so fast he ended up getting a promotion the following year and earning a lot more money. So not only was his investment in a green car pass great for making time to do his English, but it was also a great financial investment.

The point is, **find time to study**.

No excuses.

Thirty minutes to an hour a day is all you need. Any more than that, and you're probably just wasting time, anyway. Your learning should be focused and intense. We'll talk about what you might do in this time throughout this book—80% of what my boys and girls in my MEFA coaching course do is all the same, but often it's the 20% customised to you personally that has the biggest impact—but it should be the kind of study that makes your head feel like jelly when you're done.

It's simple, really: if you're not tired at the end of your study, you didn't do it right.

### *Relaxed Usage and Exposure*

Now you've got your intensive learning time scheduled, it's time to have fun with English.

Learning a language is a little like weight training (this is something I'll talk about more in Chapter 7 when we talk about building fluency faster). You've got to put that hard, intensive time into your exercises. And that's what you do in your learning time. But really the muscle growth happens during recovery: and English is similar.

You can't skip the study part, because otherwise your English will not grow and you'll end up staying in the same place forever. But the real magic happens when you then just let go of the need to learn and become an English *user*.

You can do anything you like in English, and you should do as much as you can every day.

There's only one rule: you should **NOT** do anything that you wouldn't do in your native language.

Everything you do should be real.

This is not a time for practise.

It's not a time for doing pointless things.

It's a time for doing real stuff, just like you would with your first language.

If you love watching films, watch them in English. If you read a lot of fiction (personally I'm obsessed with Scandinavian crime fiction) then read it in English. Don't stop to look up words. Don't treat it as studying. Just do it in the same way as you do your first language.

Over time, as you develop the right habits your brain gets used to the idea. And you'll stop overthinking everything as you speak and listen, you'll stop translating in your head and you'll stop feeling like English is this tiring, impossible thing to do. But again, you need to do it right.

You need to think like an English *speaker*, not like an English *learner* – if you don't, you'll just create the wrong kind of habits and make your problems worse.

You also need to remember that just using English is not enough: both of the two "tracks" are essential. Using must follow learning.

Got that?

Learn first, use second

Great.

Let's move on and start talking about *what* you should be learning in your focused study time.

## CHAPTER 5

## LEARNING ALL THE
## LANGUAGE YOU NEED

IT SHOULD BE obvious that to speak a language, you need *language*. But it's not so easy to figure out *what* language you need.

Imagine that your *Why* requires you to speak English as well as a native speaker. So let's ask how much of their language *they* actually know.

Now, this is actually a very difficult question to answer. First, because no two people are ever going to be the same. But it's even hard to define what a word really is. For example, the word "eat" is clearly a word. But how do we count "eats" or "eaten"? It seems strange to consider "eat" and "eats" as separate words, but they do have different meanings… so why not? Then what about "ate"? Its form is different to "eat", and it means something different. Should we count these as separate words? Or is it still the same word?

When we consider that most verbs have multiple forms—*eat, eats, eaten, eating, ate*—the question of how we count them is obviously very, very important. This is why you will see so many different estimates of the number of words in English.

Generally, though, we say that there are about 1,000,000 words in English. This is a good estimate, in my opinion, not least because it keeps the maths simple.

So, now that we've decided on the number of words, let's ask how many does your average John Doe native speaker know? Unfortunately, this isn't a simple question, either. Someone like me who has a PhD is obviously going to have a larger vocabulary than someone who only graduated from secondary school. Unless, of course, that person is an enthusiastic reader... in which case they may well know *more* than me.

If this discussion is starting to irritate you, welcome to the wonderful world of linguistics.

A good estimate is 25,000 words, on the assumption that the person has an undergraduate degree and has just finished university. So, we're talking about your average British 22-year-old.

Now, hang on just a minute...

That ain't many words?

Even someone as mathematically challenged as me will quickly work out that this is only 2.5% of the words in English! That's a tiny, tiny, tiny percentage.

Does this make the average person an illiterate idiot? No. It simply means that we don't actually need that many words to communicate well.

This means two important things for you: first, you obviously can't learn everything.

I mean, if native speakers only know 2.5% of the words in their language, for you to try to learn all the words is unrealistic and, frankly, stupid.

Ammon Shea, author of *"Reading the Oxford Dictionary: one man, one year, 21,730 pages"* himself says:

---

 *"As far as hobbies go, [reading the dictionary] is as most of them are – largely useless. Contrary to what many self-help books would*

*have you believe, adding a great number of obscure words to your vocabulary will not help you advance in the world. You will not gain new friends through this kind of endeavour, nor will it help you in the workplace. At best you might bore your friends and employers and at worst you will alienate them, or leave them thinking that there is something a little bit wrong with you."*

---

So there we go. Even the guy who read the entire bloody Oxford Dictionary thinks it's a waste of time. (Hint: read Shea's book instead – it's excellent. I especially like the introduction where he talks about getting blinding headaches from spending too much time reading the dictionary.)

### My Mate Vilfredo

While this is all very interesting (or at least I think it is – you can tell I'm not very popular at parties, right?), we're still stuck. Which words should you learn?

The truth is: you should focus not on individual *words*, but rather on *chunks* that show how words are commonly put together. We're going to talk about this in detail in a minute. But first I want to introduce you to my mate Vilfredo.

Vilfredo Pareto – ever heard of him?

He was a nineteenth-century Italian economist who made one of the most important discoveries of the century: *the 80/20 Principle*.

The 80/20 Principle was popularised by Richard Koch in his book "*The 80/20 Principle*" (another one that you should read), but the concept was in no way original to him.

Pareto conducted a study and found that 80% of Italy's wealth was owned by just 20% of the people. And everybody else—a massive 80% of the population— had the little bits that were leftover. The remaining 20%.

Other people got interested in this and did similar studies in other countries finding the exact same pattern. The same distribution of wealth is found everywhere: 80% of the wealth is always owned by around 20% of the people.

There are powerful reasons for this, but it's related to the (very predictable) way that people behave and the way this behaviour shapes society as a whole. Incidentally, this same reason is why communism has always failed. It's simply not in people's nature to behave in the way socialist ideology says they should.

It's not just money where we see this massive imbalance, though. It's everywhere. And importantly it doesn't have to be exactly 80/20, either. Often the imbalance will be more like 90 to 10 or even 99 to 1. But as a general rule, we say the 80/20 rule, because it's easy to remember.

What other things follow the principle?

Take a look in your wardrobe at all the clothes you own. You'll find that you wear about 20% of them 80% of the time. I used to own a ridiculous amount of clothes, before I adopted the minimalist lifestyle. I had more clothes than my ex-wife and kids put together. You should have seen my shoe cupboard!

Guess what?

I didn't wear most of them most of the time. Of all my clothes, I wore about 20% of them 80% percent of the time. So I threw 80% away—along with most of everything else I own—and now I live out of just one large bag. That's a story for another day, though.

As I write this, I'm looking down at the carpet in the Airbnb I'm currently living. Of all the space on the carpet, about 20% of it has most of the damage. The wear and tear is all in the space around my feet and the table where people sit. It's completely worn out – so thin that I can basically see the wooden floor through it. But the edges? They're like new.

In any computer software, 20% of the functions will do 80% of the work (or so I'm told).

In any activity, just 20% of the effort will give you 80% of the results. Then to get the final 20%, you've got to put in a massive 80% more effort.

This very book, for example: I wrote the first draft in a couple of afternoons (80% of the result for 20% of the time). But editing what I wrote has taken a couple of months (80% of the time for the final 20%).

I could go on giving examples all day, but I won't.

The point is, the 80/20 rule is a force of nature that can help us understand loads of different things – including how to study English most efficiently.

### *80/20 English*

The first time I came across the 80/20 rule was as memorable (and orgasmic) as the first time I had sex.

The sudden realisation that I could just cut out 80% of what I was doing…and still get most of the results.

Make sure you read Richard Koch's famous book (mentioned above), and another one I highly recommend if you're interested in marketing: Perry Marshall's "80/20 Sales and Marketing". More than Koch's book, reading Marshall's is what really made me understand the true power of the 80/20 principle.

How does all this relate to your English?

Well, of all the words, phrases, chunks, idioms, expressions, and grammar patterns that speakers know, they use just 20% of them 80% of the time.

Let me demonstrate.

I took one of my 'Extraordinary English Conversations' interviews—an interview with the CEO of a large and successful business that I did as part of a regular series of in "Extraordinary English Speakers", the MEFA graduate programme—and counted all the words. Then I ranked them from most frequent to least frequent and plotted them on a graph.

This is what I got:

———

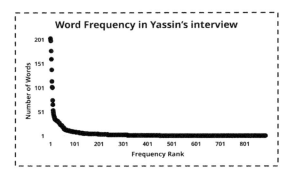

In the hour long conversation, there were 5,096 words in total, and 887 different words. So if I take the top 20% of the different words—177 words—that gives me a total of 3,887 words. Which works out as 76% of the total number of words, or close to 80%.

See what I mean?

20% of the language gets used 80% of the time. If you just learned 177 words, you'd be able to understand at least 76% of our conversation.

The point I'm trying to make here is that not all language is equal. Some items of language are infinitely more useful than others, and the more you focus your time and effort on the useful stuff, the faster your results will be.

Don't misinterpret this, though. Most people's reaction to this is to go looking for lists of the most common words, phrases and expressions in English. But actually this is counterproductive. Why? *Because those lists won't match you and your "Why".*

Remember: your goal is not to learn the whole English language, but to learn the English *you* need in *your* life and work. And that will be very different for different people.

### The Two Types of Language

Several years ago, my cheap (but long suffering) bike got damaged, and the cost of repair was going to be more than the bike was worth. So I decided to get a new one.

There's an area of Tokyo that I love called *"Yanaka"*, and every time I was there I'd seen a cool-looking bike shop – a place called *"Tokyobike"* (I've seen people riding them in London too, by the way).

It was the first time I'd ever bought a road bike—my old one was a cheap off-the-shelf model from the local supermarket—, and I rather naively thought I could just walk in, pick one, and walk out with it.

Oooooh noooo.

You pick your frame, then customise it with parts to suit. They then take your order, assemble the bike, and you pick it up two weeks later.

I walked into the shop, and the shop assistant turned to me and asked, *"Can I help you?"* (in Japanese). I tell her, *"Yes, I'd like to buy a road bike, but I'm not sure what I need."*

So far this is a very standard conversation. You could easily walk into a tailor's and ask for a new suit with the same language – *"I'd like to buy a suit, but I'm not sure what I need."*

But then the conversation turned to *brakes*, *gears*, *tires* and *saddles*.

Try walking into a tailor's and asking them to adjust your saddle – it's not going to work.

Even at my level of Japanese, this was surprisingly difficult. I knew all the basic language the lady was using, but I wasn't familiar with the names of many parts of the bike. I also didn't know what to call different types of handlebars in Japanese – for example, I wanted to ask what's the difference between a straight pair of handlebars and the rams-horn style. But I didn't know what those were called.

I got the job done in the end, but it was far from eloquent. Before I went back to collect the bike, I spent some time watching Japanese YouTube videos about bikes, bike repairs and bike shops.

I now know that those handlebars shaped like rams' horns aren't even called that in English – they're called "drop handlebars", and in Japanese *"duropu handoru"*.

The point I want you to get from this is that there are <u>two</u> types of language. **One:** Very, very common, high-utility language that gets used everywhere, in almost any kind of topic or situation **Two:** Language that only gets used in certain specific situations, such as a bike shop.

## *Type One Language*

When the shop assistant asked me, "Can I help you?" she was using Type One language. This is the true 80/20 language: It's the fundamental language that gets used in any kind of situation, again and again and again.

This is mostly going to be phrases and expressions that get used in many situations, such as: "Can I help you?" and "Yes, please." Here we will also find groups of words that are usually stuck together in a certain way.

For example, groups of words like *'the first thing...'*
This little group or **"chunk"** of words is used over and
over again:

---

- 'The first thing I do in the morning is make a
  cup of coffee.'
- 'The first thing to look for when buying a bike
  is this…'
- 'The first thing you need to do if you want to
  improve your English is this…'

---

Here's another example of a common chunk of words:
*'I'd go for…'*

Imagine we're at a restaurant: *"If I were you, I'd go for*
the curry; it's really good.*"*

But in a bike shop, the assistant might be giving you a
recommendation: "*I'd go for* twelve or sixteen gears".

Again, here we're talking about high frequency, very,
very common language: phrases, expressions and
chunks that get used in basically any kind of situation
you can imagine, all the time.

This is the most important language that you can ever learn, because once you learn it in one situation, you can apply it to loads and loads of other situations, over and over again. It is the true fluency and natural-ness building language. Focus on this type of language first and foremost.

### *Type Two Language*

When the shop assistant explained to me how to adjust the brakes, saddle and chain she was using *Type Two* language. This is language which is still quite common, but is specific to a particular situation.

In terms of the bike shop example: words like 'cog,' 'chain,' 'handlebars,' and 'saddle'. These are fairly common words, but they get used only when you're talking about bikes. You wouldn't say 'cog,' 'chain,' or 'handlebars' if you worked in finance or wanted to order a burger in McDonalds. If you are in medicine, you're probably not going to be saying 'bike saddle' every single day (however you might say "saddle sore" if you happen to get a lot of cyclists coming your way…).

For you, Type Two language will mainly be the language you need in your particular job, profession or speciality. Most people who use English at work learn this type of language quite quickly, because they run into it every day, over and over again. This is why most people find talking about their job fairly easy, but struggle with things like small talk.

### So How Many Words Should You Learn?

Now we come full circle, right back to the beginning of this chapter. What words should you learn, and how many do you need to speak English well?

By now, you should be able to see that the only realistic answer to this question is: *It depends on you and your "Why".*

Everything I've talked about in this chapter is first and foremost a mindset shift.

I *can't* point you to a list of words that you should learn and say, *"This is all you need,"* because that's bullshit. There are such lists available (the General Service List, or the Academic Words List), but these are old, based on old research, and old ways thinking.

If you need a goal to work towards, then I say aiming for the native-speaker number of 25,000 words is a good bet. Now, this is impossible to measure, and as I'm going to explain in the next chapter, focusing on individual words isn't a very good idea, anyway. So, I recommend this: aim to learn 25,000 common **chunks** of language.

To make things simple, we can say native speakers take 25 years to learn this much – so that's about 1000 items a year. That works out as 2.7 items a day.

Learn on average 3 chunks, phrases or expressions a day and you will move forward at lightning speed… *if* you learn them *well* and you focus first on Type One language, then on Type Two as a secondary thing.

Incidentally, the Weekly Lessons I make for my Extraordinary English Speakers group (the MEFA graduate programme) work on this basis. They focus on Type One language, and I aim to include, on average, about 20 items a week.

See how that works?

You don't need the lessons or materials I make, of course. I use this as an example because, obviously, materials I make are based on the principles we're discussing here. Any material will work as long as it's a source of native-like language rich in *chunks* to learn. I just make it easy by giving you materials filled with the most useful language. We'll talk more about materials in Chapter 9.

Anyway.

I keep mentioning chunks.

What are these chunks? And why should you be concentrating on them? Because this is quite a big topic—and probably the most important in this book if you struggle with fluency and naturalness when speaking, it gets the entire next chapter all to itself.

## CHAPTER 6

## LEARNING LANGUAGE FOR FLUENCY AND NATURALNESS

WHEN I WAS A TEENAGER, my family had a dog called Cassy. She was a bearded collie—a truly beautiful breed of dog—and very, very excitable. So excitable in fact, that whenever people came to visit us... *she'd end up peeing on the carpet.*

Well, that's exactly how I feel right now.

This is the part of the book I've been looking forward to. *Chunking.*

Don't worry.

I'm not going to pee on your carpet.

But I am going to geek out a bit.

Chunking is my area of speciality, along with fluency and the concept of "naturalness" – or what in Applied Linguistics is called "Nativelike Selection".

These things are exactly what *chunks* help native speakers to do. It's what I did my PhD in. And it's what you need to focus on if you want to massively increase your fluency and naturalness in English.

So why are these so-called "chunks" so important?

Well, one of my course members said:

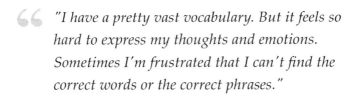

*"I have a pretty vast vocabulary. But it feels so hard to express my thoughts and emotions. Sometimes I'm frustrated that I can't find the correct words or the correct phrases."*

The key here is: *"I have a pretty vast vocabulary… but… still struggle to find the words."* People tend to be somewhat obsessed with vocabulary. I'm always hearing people say, *"If only I knew more words, I would be able to speak English more fluently."*

Is this really the case?

Most of the time, no.

Yes, knowing words is useful. But if you can under-stand most of what I'm writing here, you probably don't *need* more vocabulary. Of course, again, all else being equal, more vocabulary is better than less. Of course. That goes without saying. But the words them-selves are only <u>one</u> part of the equation.

Learning more and more words tends to end up in the category of 80% effort, but only 20% of the results. This is because—as I already demonstrated in the previous chapter—you really don't need that many words.

What is important—and almost definitely what you are failing to do now—is how you *combine* the words you've got. And in order to do that you need pretty *deep* knowledge regarding the vocabulary that you do have.

There's a famous saying in linguistics from the researcher Rupert Firth: *"You shall know a word by the company it keeps."*

What he meant by this is that in order to know a word well, you need to know what words go together with it.

A good example of this is the word 'cause'. As a verb, 'cause' means: *to bring about a result*. Something causes something else.

Simple, right?

Well, no.

Because what you can't tell from the dictionary definition is that the word 'cause' is only normally used in **unpleasant** situations. We don't use the word 'cause' in positive, happy-sounding phrases.

For example, some chunks you might see using 'cause' are: *cause of death, cause pain, cause acute discomfort, cause a problem.* You don't "cause happiness" or "cause a person to love you". These are grammatical, but they sound very, very strange.

Here are some other common chunks….

We say, "plastic surgery" and not "plastic operation."

"Good morning" sounds natural, but "Pleasant first half of the day" doesn't.

We say, "Could you help me?" and not "Could you aid me?"

These are ways in which native speakers chunk language. All the alternatives are grammatical, but for whatever reason, they're just not what people say.

They're not *chunks*.

This is important because native speakers primarily speak with chunks. Yes, we can use grammar rules and individual words to make creative sentences. We can. But most of the time we don't, simply because this is a really inefficient use of processing power.

A good analogy for chunks is the shortcut keys you have on your computer. Sure, I could click through menus to find the "save" option every time I want to save my document – but it's much faster and easier to hit "Command-S" on my keyboard.

I use the software "Premier Pro" for editing videos and took the time to learn all the shortcut keys I need. I don't actually remember how to find many of the functions I use via the complicated menu system, because why would I bother? It takes a lot of time and effort to click around looking for different functions… whereas a shortcut-key is instant.

The reason native speakers are able to sound so fluent and natural is because they *do not* construct their language using grammar rules and individual words –

they simply store chunks in memory and use them *as is*, like "language-shortcuts".

What this means for you is this: if you concentrate on learning chunks, you're going to get the same benefit from them as native speakers do. But if you study the way many people do—individual words and grammar rules—you're basically learning to compute language the hard way, and ignoring all the "shortcut keys" of English.

Or, to put it another way, it's like you're clicking around in complicated menu systems to do simple tasks that could be done instantly if only you knew the right key. Importantly, with time and practice, yes, I could get good at clicking through menu systems in Premier Pro for editing my videos. BUT: no matter how fast I get at doing this, it will <u>never</u> be as efficient as using shortcut keys. Doing it manually in the menus is limited – and this is the same for speaking. Yes, you can practise computing words in your head enough to get good at it. But all you've done is get good at a very inefficient and limited system.

### Some Different Kinds of Chunks

One of my favourite things to do when I still lived there was to sit on a bench in a busy part of Tokyo and just watch people go by. People are not just people – there are all kinds.

Young people. Old people. Rich people. Poor people. Clever people. Stupid people. People who love their jobs. People who hate their jobs. People who have lost their jobs and now have no job at all. Artists, bankers, homeless people, businessmen, chefs, designers, factory workers, carpenters, company presidents and maintenance men. People who are funny. People who are dead boring. Straight people and gay people. People who are ugly, people who are beautiful. People doing amazing things with their lives and people who hate their lives and just want to die.

In the same way, there are many kinds of chunks. Some big, some small. Some sexier than others.

My personal research focuses on a kind of chunk called a "lexical bundle" – which is the most frequent kind of chunk. This means a chunk that is several words long, and that gets pronounced as a single unit, but is not always a complete phrase (unlike an idiom or a complete expression). Good examples are things like: "in the middle of the…", "let me tell you about…", "at the end of the day…"

As I said, there are many kinds of "chunk". Here are the main, most important ones:

- **Idioms**: the cat is out of the bag; Bob's your uncle
- **Collocations**: "heavy rain" – but not "thick rain"
- **Binomials**: "fish and chips" – but not "chips and fish"
- **Phrasal verbs**: go over; get into
- **Lexical bundles**: in the middle of…, first of all…
- **Conventional expressions**: "How are you?" and "Good morning!"

The easiest ones to spot are the idioms and conventional expressions, and you will be familiar with these already.

Idioms are chunks that have a fixed meaning, normally (but not always) totally different from the literal meaning of the words. Idioms often have interesting stories behind them, too. For example, the idiom "a white elephant" refers to a gift or thing that you have been given that you don't want, but feel obliged to keep.

When I was younger, my mother had this horrible clock that my grandmother gave her. It was an antique and quite valuable, apparently. It was a huge black thing made out of stone and shaped like the Roman

Pantheon. Every hour it would chime: *gong, gong, gong, gong.* This clock was truly horrible. So my mum kept it hidden in a cupboard somewhere and only got it out when my grandmother came to visit. This is a perfect example of a white elephant.

But the idiom also has a cultural story behind it. It comes from the kings of Siam, now known as Thailand. When someone did something to upset the king, he would give them a white elephant – which they'd be burdened with. The white elephant was considered special and wasn't allowed to work. Neither could it be given away. Yet it was expensive to keep. So expensive, people given one would be ruined.

There are a lot of idioms like this in English, and the chances are you've dedicated some time to learning them. Do learn idioms. Apart from that fact that using them well will make you sound more natural—but only if used well—, they're an important part of the culture of English. This said, most idioms aren't actually *that* common. So do learn them… but make sure you learn them from real English that you hear other people use. Don't waste time with lists of idioms that you find online, because they're shit.

Lexical Bundles, on the other hand, are super high frequency. These are also the ones you want to spend most of your time and energy on learning.

### *All Chunks are Really Just Chunks*

This said: chunks are chunks.

What chunks really are is clusters of neurons in long term memory all fused together.

Although we categorise them differently, in reality there is no difference between an idiom and a "lexical bundle". Or any other kind of chunk, for that matter.

They're all just chunks. They're stored as chunks, used as chunks and understood as chunks. And you should be learning them as *chunks*.

So my advice is forget about idioms or phrasal verbs or lexical bundles or anything else… and just concentrate on learning chunks.

See language as chunks.

Speak language as chunks.

How do we do this?

Ah-ha, that's a good question. Let's talk about "data driven learning".

## *Data Driven Learning*

The next logical question then is: How do we learn in chunks?

Well, this too really is a mindset shift.

When I learned French at school, we started by learning basic sentence structure, nouns and some adjectives. We learned: "le chat" (the cat), then we were taught how to add an adjective to that: "le chat noir" (the black cat). When we learned this, I remember being interested in the fact that French puts adjectives after the noun…. Interested for all of about 5 seconds, but then I forgot about it. So in our homework when I was asked to make some examples, I made the usual mistake: I wrote something like "le blanc chien" (the white dog) and "le rouge cochon" (the red pig).

This is a really simple example, and yes, you would expect that I could remember such a simple rule. But as soon as the rules start to get even slightly compli-cated… basically *nobody* can get them right most of the time.

This is because it's not the way we actually process language. We don't process language by using rules to combine individual words. We process language in whole chunks.

There's a great scene in the film *Captain America: Civil War*. The character named "Vision" is cooking 'paprikash', a Hungarian dish. He's got a recipe in front of him, and he is following the instructions. It says, "a pinch of paprika", so he adds a pinch. He does it to make Wanda, another character (who is Hungarian), feel better. It's a nice idea, but the problem is Vision is an android and doesn't eat food. He's never eaten anything, let alone paprikash. So obviously he has no idea what it should taste like. He can only follow the rules and hope it works.

Wanda tries his cooking and says, *"I don't know what's in this… but it's not paprikash."*

Vision's cooking attempt fails.

The way language is taught in schools is like the way Vision tries to cook. It's actually backwards. You get taught grammar rules and words, then you're expected to produce language from this. But just like with cooking, this only works if you *already* know what the end result should look like.

When learning language, always go the other way.

Start with samples of real language and aim to understand and copy that sample. Never the other way around. Always chunks of real language first – then produce language based on that.

Do you remember the Two Track approach for improving your English we talked about in Chapter 4? First notice the language you don't know – in this case, notice the common chunks in samples of real conversation and **learn** them. Then **automate** what you've learned via real world use.

The key, however, is noticing the chunks. You'll never learn what you don't notice.

The big change here is not what we actually do… but rather how we look at the language. We stop looking at English as a list of individual words to memorise, and instead we focus on larger units of language. We focus on chunks.

Learning the language really can be as simple as getting a notebook and a pen and writing down the common chunks, phrase and expressions that you come across in the materials you study. Nothing here has to be complicated. Indeed, this is exactly what I do when learning languages these days. In the past, I used to use an app called "Anki" that allows you to make intelligent flashcards. The software calculates when you're likely to forget something and shows it to you at just the right time.

I don't use Anki anymore, because I find that it's too much hassle. A notebook and a pen works almost— not quite, but almost—as well.

Let's take a look at some examples.

I'm going to use samples from conversations we study in the EES Weekly Lessons (which members of my English learning community, 'Julian Northbrook's League of Extraordinary English Speakers,' get weekly as part of their membership).

I'd be lying if I said I didn't want to show these off

I put a lot of work into creating these materials, after all, so why wouldn't I want to tempt you to join the membership programme?

But I'm not trying to get you to join the group (and you can't anyway, as it's only open to graduates of my ME*F* Accelerator course). The main reason I'm using them is simply because it's hard to get permission to use samples of other people's stuff (copyright law can be a real pain in the ass).

And anyway, my materials have been optimised based on the principles we're looking at here – but look at any sample of real conversation (such as you might find in a YouTube video, for example), and you'll see exactly the same thing.

### *"Passing the Time of Day"*

The EES Weekly Lesson "Passing the time of day" is a conversation between Felix and Dan. Felix begins telling the story like this:

―――――――

It was Saturday morning and the cupboard was bare. As I locked my door, ready to set off for the supermarket, my new neighbour Dan emerged from his apartment at the same time.

"Hey! How's it going?" he asked. "How are you settling in?"

"I'm fine thanks," I replied. "I'm just off to stock up my fridge. There's nothing left…

―――――――

Notice the phrases that are used to connect with the other person and start the conversation. "How's it going?" and "How are you settling in?" are both examples of what linguists call 'phatic communication' – that is, phrases and expressions that are used to greet people, start conversations or say goodbye. In the

same way, "I'm fine, thanks," is a standard response –
because Felix understands here that Dan is not asking
about his health.

Next we get, "I'm just off to" – a very common chunk,
and "stock up my fridge", which is less common, and
considered "Type 2", but useful in this context.

The chunk "there's nothing left" is used to add expla-
nation to what he's just said.

Then, at the end of the conversation, Dan says:

------

"Give us a shout if you need anything. We must
go out for a beer some time."

"I'm up for that," I said as we went our separate
ways.

------

The phrase "Give us a shout if you need anything" is
another example of phatic communication. While Dan
probably is sincere (if Felix asks for help, Dan will give
it) this is not why he says it – rather he is indicating
that the conversation is over. The phrase "We must go
out for a beer," is a continuation of this – and in the

same way, "I'm up for that" is an acknowledgement that the conversation is over.

The point is this: when native speakers talk, they are speaking in chunks. This entire dialogue is chunked.

They are also always using chunks like this in clever ways to do things that might not be related to the literal meaning of the words. Meaning is very often found much deeper than the actual words used; you have to look at how words are used in phrases, and how phrases are used as part of the overall conversation.

### *"Damning with Faint Praise"*

When I was a university student, a friend of mine fancied a girl in our class. He was a bit shy, and not very good with girls… but we kept teasing him and telling him he should ask her out.

Then one day we were in the student bar having a couple of pints for lunch (with our tutor no less – remember, I was an art student) and this girl was there.

So my mate, he suddenly stands up, downs his drink, and announces: "I'm going to ask her out!!"

He walks right up to her and says, *"Hey, would you like to go to lunch with me tomorrow?"*

Even writing this makes me cringe, because she turned around with a cold smile on her face and said, "Sorry, I think I'm washing my hair then."

My mate was understandably devastated… though not for long, because we skipped afternoon classes and just kept drinking…

What does this even mean though: *"I think I'm washing my hair then"*?

Well, obviously she wasn't actually planning to wash her hair. That's not exactly the sort of thing we plan in advance. No. This is an expression with an idiomatic meaning – it basically means: "No way! Washing my hair is far more exciting to me than going to lunch with you."

In other words, "I'm not at all interested in spending time with you!"

This is a pretty harsh thing to say.

Here's another example of this in a different situation. A group of friends have just been to an art gallery opening party held by Jake.

The friends didn't like Jake's art, and they're joking among themselves (behind his back) about the party, and, well, being a bit mean.

Look for the example of "I think I'm washing my hair" and see how many other chunks you can spot:

---

"How was it?" Jake asked me as we were leaving.

"It was just what I expected," I said. "Definitely food for thought!"

"You must be very proud," added Dan. "I've never seen anything like it!"

"It's the first time I've been to the opening of an exhibition," said Claire. "What a different experience this evening has been."

He handed her an invitation.
"Well there's another opening next Friday, if you're interested," said Jake.

"Thanks!" she said brightly.

We collected our coats and headed for the door.
"Hmm," she said to me, as we left. "I think I
may be washing my hair that night."

---

Do you see how many chunks there are in this very
short stretch of conversation?

Like the previous dialogue, it's basically *all* chunks.

### *"Moving On"*

Here's another example of a conversation where Kemi,
the person *listening* to her friend and ex-coworker,
uses cleverly timed phrases to keep the conversation
moving forward. Tom is telling her how different his
new job (at Google) is to his old office job:

---

 "I can't begin to tell you how different it all
is," said Tom. "It took me a while to get
used to it. For a start, we can play table
tennis in the office and there's a slide,
computer games and a great canteen."

"You're having me on!" said Kemi.

"No, seriously," continued Tom. "There's also a granny flat where you can sit and relax, and—get this—a little caravan where you can have meetings."

"What on earth is the point of that?" wondered Kemi.

"It's supposed to make the staff feel more creative, apparently," said Tom. "The trouble is, with all these quirky features taking up so much of the space, it's surprisingly difficult to find somewhere quiet to think."

———

Kemi uses the underlined chunks to show she is interested in what Tom is saying, and to indicate that she wants to hear more. Really, the literal meaning of the phrases is irrelevant – what matters is the way they're used in the context of the conversation.

Again, do you see how this works?

Most of the words we see here are quite ordinary words. But it's the way these words are combined and used in conversation that matters.

This shows why concentrating on the common chunks, phrases, expressions and idioms in this conversation is *much* more effective than worrying about the vocabulary.

Fluency comes from chunks, and so does sounding natural when you speak.

So learn in chunks right from the start.

### *How Much Should You Memorise?*

I'll be totally honest: *I hate memorising stuff.*

Neither do I think it's necessary.

When I studied for the Japanese Proficiency test (which I took only because I wanted to become a translator), I worked with a tutor who had me memorise loads of example sentences.

Sure, it worked.

But it was painful as hell and I hated it.

And two months after the test I'd forgotten it all, anyway.

So give yourself a break: you don't need to memorise everything and anything. Generally, if you're struggling to remember something, it's either because it isn't useful, or because you don't understand how it's supposed to be used in context. If something is useful enough, you *will* see it again when you're reading, speaking, or listening to English.

The important thing is awareness. It's about noticing chunks and how they're used by native speakers. The more aware you become of chunks, the more they will start to stand out to you. And chunks are also highly repetitive, so just "doing" your life in English will help you to memorise them as long as you've learned them in the first place (just like we talked about in Chapter 4).

Depth of understanding is far, far more important than remembering lots of stuff you don't really know how to use. So in general there's no reason to force yourself to memorise things. Just become aware of things going on in the language samples you study and then use them.

One very, very good thing to do is extensive reading and listening. This is when you're reading or listening to English for pleasure, or to acquire some kind of information – <u>not</u> to study English. You're not stopping to look up things you don't know, or even trying to understand everything. You're just reading and listening in exactly the same way as you would in your native language.

Remember: this by itself won't work.

Just doing extensive reading and listening is very ineffective, because most people don't notice the things they need to learn.

Again, just like we talked about in Chapter 4.

But it's a fantastic way to *reinforce* your careful, analytical study. If you study the way I suggested in the last section, you'll be learning lots of very useful chunks. Then in your relaxed reading or listening time, *you'll hear those same chunks and bits of language*. When you do that, they will stand out, and you will be like, "Ah ha!! I learned that recently!"

### Good Pronunciation is Chunked

Chunks are like language-shortcut keys, and this makes them instant to say, and instant to *understand*.

It also means chunks are pronounced as single units. People who try to pronounce every word clearly and distinctly are *not* easy to understand. This is because when we speak naturally, we speak in chunks. And we understand in chunks. Naturalness is fluency for the listener and allows us to save brain-power by removing complex computation.

What this means is: if you over-pronounce every single word, it will make you *harder* to understand, not easier.

One of the reasons native speakers might sound like they speak really fast is because they "chunk" their language.

For example, a phrase such as "at the end of the day" is actually a single unit of language, so it *gets pronounced* as a single unit. So although there are six words in this phrase when we write it down, in the brain of a native speaker it functions like one word. The correct pronunciation is actually not "At. The. End. Of. The. Day", but "athendovthday".

When you pronounce this as a single unit, a native speaker will recognise it instantly. Even if you pronounced the "end" bit wrong—for example as "ond"—it would still sound natural and fluent.

On the other hand, pronouncing a chunk like this in individual words forces the listener to hear it in individual words – which makes it much harder to understand, because they have to process what you're saying in a slow, conscious way.

So when you are learning, pay close attention to the way native speakers pronounce chunks – in particular, those super-high frequency chunks that we talked about earlier.

This is another reason why you need to learn to recognise English as chunks—not words and grammar rules —and learn in this way right from the start. That way you'll also learn correct articulation from the start.

There isn't space in this book to go into the topics of accent, pronunciation and articulation in detail: but all you really need to know for now is, *English speakers speak in chunks, so you should learn in chunks and speak as they do.*

If you want to go deeper into the topic of accent, into-nation and the way you sound when you speak, pick up a copy of my book "Awesome Accent" which is all about changing the 'sound' of your English and contains a lot of exercises you can use as part of your intensive learning time.

It's available on Amazon, or go to https://doingenglish.com/awesome-accent.

## CHAPTER 7

## HOW TO SOUND GOOD AND NOT BE BORING

I HATED writing essays when I was an art student. But more than writing them, I hated knowing I had an essay to write.

Not wanting to leave it to the last minute, I'd head straight to the university library to write.

Writing these essays was painful.

I had no idea what to write. So I had to really force myself to do it.

After hours and hours of work and frustration, I'd reach the word limit and consider myself finished.

Do you think I got good grades for these?

Of course I didn't!

My grades were awful.

Until one day when we got an essay on a topic I was really interested in. This time I didn't go straight to the computer to write. Instead, I read books and watched videos on the topic. Then, when it was time to write, the words just flowed. I finished in half the time it normally took, got a great grade, and most importantly, for the first time I was pleased with what I'd written.

This sounds kind of obvious, but you can't talk about a topic you don't know anything about. Simply put, if you don't know jack shit about a topic…you're not going to be able to speak about it well, no matter how good your language skills are.

For example, I'm extremely knowledgeable in two very different areas: applied and psycholinguistics, and direct response marketing.

An odd combination, I know.

But whatever.

When it comes to how the human brain acquires and processes language, I could talk non-stop for hours, because I have a huge amount of knowledge on the topic. I can talk about it in English, and in Japanese, completely fluently.

A lot of Japanese people, however, won't be able to talk about psycholinguistics fluently (or probably at all), because they don't know anything about it.

When it comes to something like law, on the other hand, I'm just as clueless. A friend of mine recently graduated from the same university where I did my PhD. She's a non-native speaker, and yes, she studied law. She can talk about this topic much more fluently than I can, because she has a greater depth of knowledge. She knows what she's talking about!

When people say, "Oh, my mind went blank!" sometimes it's because they don't know the chunks they need… but sometimes it's because they really don't know what to say. This is a problem of knowledge, not a problem of language.

Knowledge underlies everything that you talk about. Now, in work situations, I think this is kind of obvious, and also not really a problem. The chances are, if you're in a certain profession, you already know enough about that profession.

If you're a doctor, you probably know lots about medicine; you probably don't need to learn more about it. If you're an IT professional, you know lots about your field. You're a professional! So of course you do.

It seems obvious, but a lot of people miss this. Sure, you can spend a lot of time memorising lists of random vocabulary words. But what are you going to do with that vocabulary, if you have no knowledge of the topics where it's relevant? So dedicate time to just doing things, having exciting experiences and collecting knowledge of things that you can talk about.

Yes, of course learning bits of English is an important part of getting really good at speaking English. But learning about the world and life is also important. Experience drives learning, and it also drives the conversations we have.

Dedicate time to doing things. To getting interesting content, filling your head up with stuff to talk about. Sometimes the best thing you can do for your English is go to the cinema and watch an interesting film; go to an art gallery and see a great exhibition; or get on the train and go somewhere you've never been before.

You might not learn much language (maybe none, if it's in your native language), but it will give you topics to talk about.

And honestly?

If you've got interesting things to say, people will forgive your language mistakes. Probably they won't even notice them.

Not so if you've got nothing to say.

People with nothing interesting to say are boring, no matter how fluent they are.

### Having Stories to Tell

About 17 years ago, I went to China.

I was staying in Hong Kong for five weeks to take photographs and research the art there. While I was there, I decided to travel to a city called "Guangzhou" to visit the Guangzhou Art Museum.

At the time I was a student and had very little money, so I booked my hotel based on the low price. The hotel was on the opposite side of the city, but, *no problem*, I thought. I could just take the train. I'd been taking trains everywhere in Hong Kong with no problems at all.

I took a taxi from Guangzhou central station to the hotel where I was staying. Then, the next morning, I got up bright and early to go to the Guangzhou Art Museum.

I didn't have a laptop, internet access or anything like that. And this was the world before smartphones, remember. All I had was a small guidebook that didn't even give proper instructions on how to get to the museum. The only thing I knew was the name of the train stop I needed.

I headed to the nearest underground station… and that's when it hit me.

Underground stations in Guangzhou were totally different to the ones in Hong Kong. There was no English on the train maps. I don't know if this is still the case: remember, this was quite a long time ago now.

I bought a ticket from a machine—pretty much by pressing buttons randomly—and went to the plat-form… but I had no idea where to go, or even what train to get on. I knew the name of the station I needed – but I couldn't read any of the signs. And my guide-book only had English.

So I did what any other lost tourist would do – I asked the guard in the train station.

*"Excuse me, do you speak English…?"* I asked.

No response.

*"Excuse m…"*

I didn't finish repeating myself, because right then the guard did something *shocking*. He just put his hand in my face and refused to speak to me.

Not exactly helpful.

So, I did the only thing I could. I left the station, pulled out my trusty tourist map… and started to walk. Of course, even with a map I got really lost, and it took me more than 5 hours to get the art museum (and it still took 3 hours to get back on the way home!).

You know what though?

That walk turned out to be the best experience I had on my entire trip to Hong Kong and China. I saw so many interesting things that you just wouldn't normally see. Things that aren't in tourist guides. Everyday life.

It also turned out that I went during the Mid-Autumn Festival. There were all these beautiful hand-crafted lamps everywhere. I walked through back streets (probably not a safe thing to do) and parks and all kinds of different areas.

And yes, I got stared at a lot.

Imagine: an English kid in a punk-band t-shirt wandering around the streets of Guangzhou. But it was a fantastic experience. And although the art museum itself was fascinating, the walk there was definitely the best part.

The point of this story is this: *the best conversation topics we have are our own stories* – and these only come from doing things and experiencing the world. What started off as a negative experience actually gave me a really great story to tell.

During that walk, there was one experience in particular that stuck with me. I was walking up the street and went past a noodle shop. A lady stood outside, and she called me over and practically dragged me into her shop. No problem, I was hungry anyway.

I was sat at a table right in the middle of the shop, surrounded by old men who stared at me.

I felt like an animal in a zoo.

Nobody could speak English, and I couldn't speak Chinese. So I just let the lady give me anything she wanted.

I'm still not exactly sure what it was that I ate.

But it was good. *Really* good.

At first the woman gave me a spoon, but the thin, stringy noodles were impossible to eat like that. So I gestured for chopsticks. The old men cheered and then laughed when I couldn't use them, either.

I paid, and left.

That was it.

In total the experience lasted about 15 minutes. But it has always stuck with me, and it's a story I've shared many, many times.

Sometimes you just don't need language. Probably if I'd been able to speak Chinese, it wouldn't have been such a memorable experience.

Fundamentally, people are people.

We have very different cultures, ways of thinking and ways of speaking. But we're all people. For just 15 minutes, I felt like that lady and the old guys in the shop were my best friends.

The point I'm trying to make here is that English is, first and foremost, about life. I've already argued that English itself is not useful – what matters is what you *do* with it. Your *Why*. But it goes the other way, too. The more you do, the more useful your English will be: experience drives learning.

So actively set out to experience life. Collect experiences and then tell your stories.

## Using English as a Tool for Self-Education

Shakespeare was a clever guy, and by all accounts a great businessman.

He said a lot of great things, and we can learn a lot from his life and work. But here's one of the best: *"Ignorance is the curse of God; knowledge is the wing wherewith we fly to heaven."*

What Shakespeare meant here is that the key to success in life is *constantly educating yourself.*

More than 50% of the internet is still in English. So unless you speak Russian (6.5%), Japanese (5.6%), German (5.5%), or Spanish (5.1%), it's going to be pretty hard to find anything much in your own language.

Everybody's always talking about needing a native speaker to practise with. Well, if you want to use your English, why not open a book? Or take an online course?

Remember: experience of and with language can come in all kinds of ways. One of the best things you can do for your English—and for yourself—is to learn about some other topic in English.

Here's a little story that illustrates this well, even if it is a little cheesy: once upon a time, there was a bird. He was watching a bee work.

The bee worked hard making honey, but the bird knew the bee could not keep the honey. Soon the humans would come and take it.

The bee flew by the bird.

"Hey!" shouted the bird. "Heeeeeeey Bee!!"

"Let me ask you a question," the bird said.

"You make honey all day long. You work so hard. But then humans steal all your honey. Don't you feel sad? Don't you feel angry? Doesn't it piss you off?!"

The bee replied, "Never."

"Never?! How can you say such a thing! You must be so angry!" said the bird.

"No, not really," replied the bee. "Humans may be able to steal my honey... but they can never steal the art of making honey. That is what matters most to me," buzzed the bee.

Pretty clever for a bee.

The bee knows that the most important thing we have can never be taken from us. Knowledge. Our own intellectual property.

When I was a student, my house got robbed. I lost my laptop and my camera – things that were very expensive for me at the time. But those things don't matter so much. Because I still had the ability to use a camera. And the knowledge and skill to make the money I needed to replace what I'd lost.

Nobody, and I mean *nobody,* can ever take that.

Remember this: The best investment you can ever make is in your own knowledge and skills. That is something which will stay with you forever. Not only that, but something like English can be used *now* to make your life easier and get more of the things you need.

Money?

English can help you get that.

Time?

English can help you get that too. If you've ever spent an hour composing one email, only to get a reply almost instantly you'll know what I mean.

Energy?

Getting good at English means the times you use English will be faster, easier and more efficient.

Imagine that you lose the ability to do business or sell your services in your own country. No problem – you can sell to the rest of the world. Or how about this? Imagine that you need to learn a skill, fast... let's say, Photoshop. Or let's make it even more specific: using Photoshop to make graphic novels.

Well guess what?

There are lots of brilliant tutorials online, and if your English is good enough, you can take a course about creating graphic novels from the University of Colorado... for free, via Coursera.

Can you see now how English is not only something you can never lose but also something you can use to change your life?

## CHAPTER 8

## THE BIG "C" OF SPEAKING WELL

When I was fourteen years old, I went on something called the French exchange. A French student came and stayed at my house for two weeks, then I went and stayed at his. So it was a kind of homestay exchange.

There's a good chance you had something like this at your school. (One of the schools I taught at in Japan had a sister-school in Australia and did an "Australian Exchange.")

Now, when I said I wanted to do the exchange, my teachers were really surprised. I was the laziest student at the school. I didn't study. I didn't participate. I didn't do anything. But when they said, *"Two weeks in France,"* I thought, *"Great! I get two weeks off school."*

So, for totally the wrong reasons, I applied. And for some reason I still don't understand even now, I got a place (which pretty much confirmed my suspicions that my teachers were all stupid).

Several months later – there I was, in France, with a host family who thought I was there to practise my French.

The only French I knew was, *"Bonjour,"* and for some reason *"mon petit cochon"* (my little pig). At a stretch, I could combine them to say: *"Bonjour, mon petit cochon!"*

The amazing result of three years of French education.

So what was I going to do in France?

Work hard and try to learn the language?

Like buggery was I.

Remember – I was only there to get out of school for two weeks. I didn't even try. I spent the whole two weeks speaking to my host family in English.

At first they were kind of surprised, but they soon got the idea. Well, they got loads of English speaking practise, and I didn't have to make any effort to learn French. So everybody was happy…apart from my teachers.

My host mother spoke English pretty well, but something about the way she spoke was… I don't know… *odd*.

Even then I was quite aware that the way she spoke English was very different from the way that people in the UK spoke English. But it wasn't that she spoke bad English. She made mistakes with her grammar and sometimes pronounced things wrong. But those things were very minor. Rather, there was something else about her English that wasn't quite right. Not the way she said things, but *what* she said, and the assumptions that she seemed to make.

At the time I didn't really understand it, but it was like we were on a different wavelength – speaking the same language, but not really connecting.

The way that people in France think is very different from the way that British people think.

The values my host family had—both cultural and personal—were quite different from my own. The result was the way they spoke was very different from the way I spoke.

Then years later when I met my wife (who was Japanese), I noticed the same thing with her. And I noticed it again with my students after I went to Japan and started teaching English. Then again after I moved to Ireland.

The way people think about improving their English tends to be too simplistic. They need to improve, so they concentrate all their time on learning the language.

While this is important, the language itself is only surface-level. Remember the LKC Triangle. You need three things to speak a language well – the Language, Knowledge of the things you want to speak about, and *Culture*.

Culture is the "Big C" of language learning.

### *Put on Your Culture Glasses*

Elton John supposedly owns more than 250,000 pairs of sunglasses. Whether it's a pair of standard black glasses, ones with blue, green or pink lenses, or even glasses with red heart-shaped lenses… *Elton has them*.

Clearly his face looks different depending on which glasses he wears. But importantly, the way the world looks to him also changes.

Slip on a pair of red glasses, and the world looks hot and passionate.

Change them for a pair with blue lenses, and the world takes on a cool-blue icy feel.

You may not have noticed, but you are wearing a pair of tinted glasses, too. Unlike all the pairs Elton has though, your glasses were put on in the months after your birth – and they can never be taken off (not fully, anyway). I call these your "**culture glasses**."

These are the lenses through which you see and understand the world. Depending on where in the world you were born and among what kind of people, you'll have a different pair of culture glasses to someone else. Everything we see, hear, do and perceive is filtered by these glasses. And just as the world looks different when you look through a pair of green lenses compared to orange ones, the way different people understand the world is different depending on their culture.

Do you remember the story I told you right at the beginning of this book? I was at a tiny car park-cafe in the Japanese countryside, and the lady in the cafe asked me if I could speak Japanese. I said, *"A little, but I'm still learning"*.

That was a lie, given that at that point I was working for a company and doing business in Japanese and had already worked as a translator. Clearly I knew more than "just a little". But to understand why I said this, and why boasting about my Japanese ability would have been a terrible idea, we need to consider *culture.*

Japanese culture values—above all else—modesty. Therefore, boasting about your own language skills is not the done thing. Saying, *"Yes, I speak excellent Japanese!"* would have (ironically) made me look like a beginner.

Cultural values like this run deep.

Very, very deep.

Japanese has a complicated social system: there are multiple levels of politeness within Japanese, and the way you speak depends on the relationship you have with the listener. For example, the word "eat" is *"taberu"* in Japanese, and if you wanted to say to a friend or co-worker "Please eat this", you could say *"tabete kudasai"*. But if you were asking the same thing of someone with a higher social status (your boss, for example), this would be considered a little rude. There's a form of language called *"keigo"*, which liter-ally means "respect language" and you'd be expected to use that. Similarly, if you wanted to say "I'll eat this", you could say *"tabemasu"*, but again, this would be a little rude if the person you're talking to is of higher status. Instead you'd say *"itadakimasu"* – which is still the word for "I'll eat", but this time it's said in a form of language called *"kenjogo"*, which literally means "humble language". If it sounds complicated, it is.

Here's another example from Japanese culture. Recently, Nana posted the following in the EES discussion group:

> *I had my first ever job interview in English today and I noticed a bad habit throughout the interview (actually I was told by the interviewer). When I answer questions I tend to do it in a negative way. This is common for people from certain countries like Japan. I couldn't believe how naturally I speak in such a negative way!*

This is a perfect example of the way culture affects the way we speak. Remember: in Japanese culture, modesty and humbleness are considered very important personal traits, and when asked about their own abilities, people will play them down, and speak quite negatively about themselves. This is a problem in situations like the one Nana describes – because the interviewers are looking at the world through their own, very different cultural values.

You hear humility, they hear a lack of confidence.

Now, luckily for you, English doesn't have a social system nearly as complicated as Japanese. But I'm telling you about this to demonstrate how deeply connected culture and language are.

Jurate, an EES member and manager at a company in the UK, told me she needs to give feedback to her team members as part of her job. When the team member has done well, this is relatively straightforward. But what if he or she has been lazy and keeps coming to work late?

In British corporate culture, direct negative feedback is frowned upon, and it isn't appropriate to say, *"You're fucking lazy and you're doing a shit job – fix your attitude or piss off"*. Instead you're expected to communicate the same meaning using indirect, often positive language. It's not surprising that this can be quite tricky to do well (I'm not very good at it – I'm far too blunt for that). But the point is, this is a function of *culture.*

When you're obviously learning the language, people can be quite kind. They will accept your mistakes. And when you say something strange, they will think, "She didn't mean to say that." But when you start to get good, things change. Suddenly, people can't understand why you say strange things, or make mistakes. They assume your level is beyond that, therefore you must have meant to say what you said.

Recently I heard a story about a woman who learned French. She was living in France, and every day she travelled to the same place by train to work.

She would walk up to the ticket office window every day and say in flawless French, *"A single ticket, please."*

She'd get the ticket and leave.

The next day, she goes to the same ticket window and asks the same person the same thing.

"A single ticket, please."

The next day the same happens.

And the next.

But then on the fifth day, something shocking happens – just as she's about to say, "A single… " the woman at the ticket window angrily says, *"Bonjour?!?!!!!"*

You see, in France, transactions such as this are supposed to start with *"Bonjour"*. Not saying it makes you rude. This isn't the case in English…at least not in the UK. We wouldn't bother saying *"Hello"* every time.

I heard a very similar story from someone in Canada who went to France. He speaks fluent French, but once in a shop he said, *"Excuse me…"* to ask a question, and was told, *"Bonjour!? In France, we don't help people who are rude."*

When it comes to simple grammar and vocabulary mistakes, people often don't even notice. And even if they do, they don't actually care. Cultural mistakes, on the other hand, can really upset people.

### Common Knowledge Is Uncommon

Something I noticed very, very quickly after going to Japan is that "common knowledge" is not the same thing in England as it is in Japan. A great example of this is catching a cold. In England, if you catch a cold, people don't normally go to the doctor to get medicine.

People in Japan, however, normally do go to the doctor when they catch a cold.

Different culture, different way of doing things.

In Japan, it's perfectly fine to ride your bike on the pavement. In the UK, a bike has to cycle on the road or in a dedicated bike lane. Again, different country, different way of doing things.

Cultural differences of this kind are important because they affect what is appropriate to say. One of the EES member lessons is called "Pedal Power", and it's about a Japanese expat living and working in London. He decides to save money by cycling to work and goes to a bike shop. When the shop assistant asks him, "Do you need a helmet?" the Japanese man replies, "No, I'll be perfectly fine cycling on the pavement." If he had known that it's illegal to do that, he would never have said this.

Cultural differences are also very common in working situations.

In Japan, people tend to do a lot of overtime, and people who don't may even miss out on important promotions because they're viewed as not putting enough time and effort into the company. In the UK, on the other hand, if you're doing overtime on a regular basis, your boss is likely to question your ability to do your job properly and call you in to talk about what problems you might be having.

When I first started teaching at school in Japan, I had to take a one-day training course. The training had basically nothing to do with teaching English. Instead, we were taught how not to upset the schools so that the company didn't look bad.

Fair enough, I guess.

Foreign teachers in Japan are very, very good at upsetting the schools they work for (because sadly, most never bother to try to learn about Japanese culture).

The first thing I learned about (and in fact the main part of the training) was the difference between *tatemae* and *honne*.

This is how my trainer explained it: *The Japanese teachers will tell you, 'You are an amazing teacher!' But it's not true.*

Honestly.

That's exactly what he said.

This is what he meant: *You will get praised… but it's a cultural thing. They feel obliged to be polite. They might say you're great even if they think you're terrible. So don't let it go to your head.*

*Tatemae* means something like "a person's public face" and *honne* means "a person's true feelings". In Japanese culture, it's considered important to be polite in public, even if you're not expressing your true feelings. Many Western people have a huge problem with this because they think it's shallow and fake. We even have a word for it: "two-faced"; a word with a very negative nuance.

On the other hand, my Japanese friends have often said that Western people come across as selfish and too full of themselves.

Neither is right nor wrong.

Both groups of people are wearing totally different "culture glasses".

Japanese culture—like many other Asian cultures— gives priority to the harmony of the group, first and foremost. It's not considered appropriate to express your personal opinions at every possible opportunity, because that might easily upset the group dynamic.

In Western societies, however, the priority tends to be placed on the individual – and people are far more concerned about expressing their own individuality than they are with preserving group harmony.

Again, neither way is right or wrong.

Just different.

### The Problem of Humour

I think anybody speaking a second language has had the experience of telling a joke they thought was really funny… only to get blank stares.

I'll never forget walking to the school where I was working one rainy morning, and greeting another teacher by saying in Japanese, *"Beautiful day!"* She looked at me like I was a total idiot. Not exactly my smoothest moment with the ladies.

In the UK we like to use this kind of ironic, sarcastic language.

Not so in Japan.

Co-workers in the UK also often swear and take the piss out of each other in the office, but there are very important (and deep) social aspects to this. Swearing, done well, is a way to bond and strengthen relationships. But I don't recommend you do it until you fully understand the social dynamics. They're complex, and again, unless you fully understand them, you run the risk of getting it horribly wrong. This is another topic I've covered extensively in my EES group.

That humour doesn't translate well between English and Japanese is obvious (the languages are so different, after all). But what you might not know is that often humour doesn't even translate well between different English-speaking cultures, either.

I forget where I read this, but there's a great story about a British guy who'd just had a meeting with an American client. The meeting had gone really well, and afterwards they went out for a drink. The American said, *"This was a very productive day! We achieved a lot."* Then the British guy responded, *"Yeah, it was pretty good. But it would have worked out a lot better if you weren't American."* Understandably, the American client was very upset – it was a pretty stupid thing to say, after all. But in British English, this kind of dry, sarcastic joke is very normal. It's how we speak, and, again, it's a part of how we bond with people. Take a look at my Facebook profile one day and see all the horrible things my friends and I say to each other. You'd think we hated each other – but on the contrary, it's precisely because we're close friends that we speak like this.

In general, Americans tend to say exactly what they mean (not so with the British). If you think about the history of America, this makes a lot of sense. It is a country that was originally made up of immigrants from different cultures. If people didn't speak in a straightforward way, other people wouldn't have understood them. So people developed a very direct "what we say is what we mean" manner of speaking. The UK never had this problem – or at least, not to the same extent.

Japan is an island country, just like the UK. However, unlike the UK, it was closed for a very long time. The Japanese language developed while Japanese people were communicating only with other Japanese people. The result is a language totally the opposite to American English: the way people speak tends to be indirect and subtle, so it requires a lot of "reading between the lines." In other words, you often have to figure out what someone means by what they *don't* say. Yet people understand each other perfectly well. A language can develop this way only when everyone shares a common cultural understanding.

When it comes to humour and being funny in English yourself, as well as swearing, my advice is: Be careful! Watch what other people do, get a feeling for the way they speak and the humour they use. Then copy that (assuming you're in the same position as them, of course – you can't copy what close friends do if you're not a close friend).

## *Learning Culture for Effective International English*

Clearly culture is a very important part of speaking well. Indeed, it is culture that defines *what* you say.

The good news is that in order to speak really great English, you don't actually need to do much extra work.

Of course, where you can, it's good to actively learn about the cultures of people you're going to be speaking English with. If you're being sent to India on a business deal, you'd do well to familiarise yourself with Indian culture before you go. When I went to Canada not too long ago, I spent a couple of hours reading up on cultural differences between the UK and Canada. This stuff doesn't have to take a lot of time because more often than not, simply showing that you've made an effort is enough. Problems arise when you completely ignore other people's way of thinking and expect them to conform to yours.

So most of the time, it's enough simply to be aware of how important culture is. This is a recurring theme throughout this book: it's all about *shifting your mindset*.

If you're *aware* of the fact that we're all wearing these "culture glasses," you'll keep an open mind, and you'll learn to notice differences. When someone says something you find offensive… just remember they probably don't mean it like that.

Always ask yourself: *"Is it possible they mean something else? Am I misinterpreting what they said?"*

Of course there are things you can do to prepare yourself (and I dare say, broaden your horizons at the same time).

Reading fiction is a great way to learn about culture. For example, I recently read two separate crime fiction series – Jo Nesbo's "Harry Hole" series, and Qiu Xiaolong's "Inspector Cao" series.

In a way, the two series are quite similar. They're both about detectives who investigate murders. Both main characters—Harry Hole and Chen Cao—are somewhat unconventional and odd in the way they do things. But the cultural settings of the books are totally different: Nesbo's books are set in Oslo, Norway, and very much reflect the Norwegian way of thinking and life. Xiaolong's books are set in Shanghai, China, and talk extensively about China and Chinese politics. The point is: almost any work of fiction will teach you a lot about that country's culture, simply because culture is the background for *everything* we do, and every story we tell.

You can also learn about culture from watching films. In fact, when I first started teaching at secondary school in Japan, for about six months I binged on every film and TV drama I could find that was set in schools. These exposed me to the culture of Japanese schools. They also gave me something to talk about with students, because often the TV shows I was watching were very popular (the 'Knowledge' aspect of the LKC Triangle – Chapter 7).

Finally, of course, getting out there and doing more is going to help. Experience drives learning. So go out, experience more, notice things, and learn from your experience.

### *A Final Note…*

This isn't something I have space to go into detail with, but being aware of a culture does not necessarily mean you will always follow it. This is something you've got to be very, very careful with—and in fact I don't really even recommend you do this—but sometimes it is more effective to go against or *defy* the culture of the people you are talking to.

For example, in business situations I tend to ignore the social ladder that I talked about before: so I talk to people as if they were on the same level as me. I don't talk *up* to people who are socially superior, and I don't talk *down* to people who are below me on the ladder.

There's a good reason for this, though.

I've consistently found that I don't work well with the kind of people who easily get upset by my not using the proper "respect language." My way of working is blunt, to-the-point and totally no-bullshit. So by talking in a frank, matter-of-fact way, I effectively filter out people who are a bad fit for me. This works for me because of the way my business is. It wouldn't have worked when I was employed in a Japanese company.

We'll talk more about this in the final chapter. But again, this is something you have to be very, very careful with.

The important thing is: if you do break the rules, you should know what the rules are and be very aware of what you're doing. There's a big difference between someone who decides to talk in a certain way because it's effective, and someone who simply doesn't know what they're doing.

## CHAPTER 9

# MATERIALS MATTER

How important are the materials you study?

The answer is simple: **very** important.

People tend to talk a lot about 'method' and learning exercises and fluency building techniques and all that stuff… but they don't talk much about the materials you learn from.

Which is silly, really.

Because if you think about it, no matter how good the method you use is, if you're learning the wrong things you're not going to improve your English much, anyway.

The "Two Track Approach" works extremely well when done properly… but it's still a total waste of time putting all that focused, intensive effort into growing your English if you're filling your head with useless crap.

Conversely, even if your method is less than ideal but the language you're learning is super useful and exactly what you need... then you're going at least get something useful.

Of course, the fastest results come from using a great method **AND** the best materials for you – but the materials are arguably more important than the method.

### *Shit Recipe, Shit Food*

Think of it like this: if you give an amazing chef a shit recipe, the food he cooks will be shit. It doesn't matter how great his cooking utensils or chopping technique is. The dish he makes is going to be crap. Because the recipe is crap.

Imagine a brussel sprout pizza with a fish-paste base instead of tomato sauce.

Sounds disgusting, right?

Jamie Oliver and Gordon Ramsey could team up and spend a month making the damn thing… but it'd

STILL be horrible. Because the recipe is the base – the sample. What the food is ultimately supposed to look and taste like. And if what the food is supposed to look and taste like is a "brussel sprout 'n' fish-paste pizza", you're doomed.

On the other hand, if you give a mediocre chef an amazing recipe (say, a classic bangers 'n' mash in onion gravy) the chances are he'll be able to make something fairly good. Not because he's amazing, but because the base is good.

When it comes to the EES member lessons, we have a system—a Method—that we use and follow. But the most important part is, ultimately, the materials. These are the sample of language that you put into your head, learn and use. That's the base. And what you are ultimately going to produce yourself.

## *Textbooks*

You probably know this, and I've talked about it already in this book, but I used to teach English at secondary school in Japan.

Every Monday afternoon myself and several other westerners—all English teachers at schools in the city where I worked—would get together for a meeting. One of the topics that came up quite a lot in our conversations was how crap the textbooks we all used were.

We'd laugh at the unnatural dialogues. The weird examples. And it did seem funny… until I realised: *we're actually wasting our students' time with this shit.*

And it is shit.

Total and utter bullshit, to the extent where it pisses me off.

But it's this experience that got me interested in the materials you learn from. So in the first year of my PhD course, I decided to focus my research on textbooks and I analysed the language used in those Japanese secondary school English teaching materials.

They're the first 'official' books Japanese students use. And everyone has to use them. So you'd expect them to be well researched and well written. What I found, though, was quite the opposite.

If you only consider the *words* in those English textbooks, they're actually okay.

Not amazing.

But okay.

But the problem is how those words are combined. The textbooks are full of chunks – but <u>not</u> the ones native speakers actually use in real conversations.


### "How many CDs do you have?"

Remember my recipe analogy?

Textbooks are often "sprouts 'n' fish-paste pizza". The most common phrase in the Japanese secondary school English textbooks books is: *"How many CDs do you have?"* (incidentally this became the title of my PhD thesis).

If you look at native speaker language, this phrase doesn't exist.

Yes, it is *possible* that someone might ask this.

Yes.

It is grammatical.

But in data banks containing billions of words, this phrase doesn't appear at all. Not even once. This is hardly surprising, because it'd need to be a pretty special situation for you to ask someone "How many CDs do you have?" – for example, you walk into someone's house and every wall is completely covered with CD shelves and there are more CDs than you've ever seen before… but even then I'd probably say, "Damn! That's a lot of CDs!!". And I wouldn't actually be looking for an answer even if I did ask, "How many CDs do you have?" – it would be used in a rhetorical sense to express my surprise and awe at so many CDs.

Even if we treat it as a frame: "how many ____ do you have?" it's still very rare – and really, the only frequent alternative is, "How many kids do you have?" Which is obviously not very useful to teenagers.

The point is, the materials you use <u>must</u> accurately represent how language is ACTUALLY used. If they don't, you're simply filling your head with garbage at best, and importantly, you could also be damaging to your English intuition long term.

### Garbage In, Garbage Out

In one of my main research projects (which is published in the top journal in Applied Linguistics) I tested a group of secondary school students on chunks taken directly from their textbooks, using special fluency-measuring techniques.

And guess what I found?

The students were fluent in textbook language.

You'll remember from Chapter 6 that native speakers store chunks in long-term memory. This is how they speak so fluently and naturally. And my research found the SAME thing in low-level, beginner English learners in secondary school. This is a huge result. All this time people have been saying that students in Japan study English for so long, but never get good... but that's bullshit! They do get good. They get good at exactly what they're taught – *useless language that nobody uses.*

In computer science there's a saying: "garbage in, garbage out". This means that if you give a computer flawed programming input, it'll give you flawed output. Garbage in, garbage out.

Language is the same.

After that study, I did a follow-up study testing Japanese adults on their ability to judge how natural-sounding English sentences are. And it turns out that their judgement is confused by their knowledge of that 'textbook language'. A massive *fifteen-years* after finishing secondary school.

What this means is, not only do materials matter for learning the English you actually need... but using the wrong materials is probably harmful long term.

## *I Will Be Confusing You with This Lesson*

There is a well-known phenomenon in linguistics research where people creating 'grammaticality tests' (tests which show people sentences and ask them if they are grammatical or not) very quickly lose the ability to accurately judge the sentences themselves. They spend so long thinking of ungrammatical sentences that those sentences start to sound natural.

This is the same thing as when you study unnatural learning materials. The reason it happens is because of the way the brain works.

In cognitive psychology, this thing is called the 'mere exposure effect' – it's the same phenomenon as when you eat something for the first time and don't like it… but after you try it a few times, you start to like it (we say that thing is an "acquired taste"). It's also why you have a preference for things which are familiar.

The problem with how language learning materials are traditionally designed is they start with grammar rules or words. Then the writer makes up an example. Most of the time these examples aren't natural or common examples of English, though, because the writer just guesses.

As an example, I Googled "future progressive tense" and found a video that I will leave unnamed (but you'll be able to find it if you want to).

Here are the first few lines of dialogue:

---

Hey Marissa, what are your plans for Friday?

Hey Hievda! I will be shopping on Friday to buy my sister a present. How about you?

I will be working on my Science report and I will be working on my English essay.

Will you be watching the new Mission Impossible movie out on Saturday?

No, I will not be watching the movie, since I have so much work to do. Sam and I will be watching the movie on Saturday.

---

There's more... lots more.

But I'll spare you.

It doesn't get any better.

Now, apart from the fact this dialogue is fucking weird, it has a serious problem: even though it demonstrates the future progressive, *it messes up your perception of how it's used*.

The future progressive is a very uncommon tense – if you count all the verbs in a natural conversation, only 0.002% of them are in the future progressive tense. But in this conversation, it's used again and again and again – something like 90% of the time.

Studying this shit ruins your intuition.

It makes you believe using the future progressive again and again and again sounds natural... which makes YOU sound UNnatural. And the worst part? You THINK you sound good... and can't hear how weird you sound.

Now, this doesn't mean making mistakes is a problem.

That's not what I'm talking about.

As long as you notice your mistakes and learn from them, it's fine. But studying bad, unnatural materials like this will make it much harder to notice your mistakes.

The first thing to look for in good materials is that they are representative of real language. Good intuition about what is—and is not—natural English comes from learning natural English over time.

Now, at this point you may be wondering if "authentic" materials—as in stuff designed for native speakers—is better.

Sometimes yes.

But sometimes no.

### Are 'Real' Materials Better?

Are "real" materials better than materials designed for language learners? By this, I mean things taken from stuff designed for native speakers: YouTube videos, podcasts, TV shows, films and the like.

The answer is yes.

And no.

OK, so I know that doesn't make sense.

Let me explain.

First, when designed properly learner-materials **ARE** real English. That is, good materials are just as authentic as any other sample of English you might find. The only difference is they have been designed for learning, which makes them easy to use.

When I make my EES member lessons—like the samples I showed you in Chapter 6—we're writing real conversations. I then take those conversations and optimise them.

A lot of time goes into checking the frequency of chunks that appear in what we write to make sure they're natural and distributed correctly (i.e. you won't see the future progressive tense used again and again, because native speakers rarely use it… but you will see it used 0.002% of the time).

Real English is great.

Especially for learning Type Two vocabulary about very specific topics. And real stuff like TV and films are certainly better than badly designed learning materials. Bad design and inauthentic data (i.e. the sample of language you put in your head) can, as I've said, damage your ability to recognise and use natural English.

So yes, learning everyday conversation—whether for day-to-day life, for business or whatever—from things like YouTube videos, podcasts and films is better than learning from shit textbooks.

However, there is a downside.

The downside is, learning from things like TV and films can be extremely slow because they're not optimised for language learning.

There used to be a great series of TV adverts for 'Fairy Washing-up Liquid' – the stuff you use to wash your dishes.

Their whole USP (unique selling proposition) was that you only needed a tiny bit of liquid... just a little goes a long, long way. The advert would show someone using normal liquid and squeezing out half a bottle and not getting many bubbles. Then, they'd compare that with Fairy – just a couple of tiny drops would produce a mountain of bubbles and get all the dishes clean.

Perhaps they still have these adverts?

I don't know.

I haven't had a TV for a very, very long time.

But those bubbles are your English.

And good learning materials are like Fairy Washing-up Liquid. Because they're optimised, you can learn a LOT from a tiny bit... *very quickly*. Whereas 'real' stuff is like the standard liquid. It's not that it doesn't work… it does. It will clean your dishes. But you need a load of the bloody stuff to get the job done well. And exercises like dictation—more on this in Chapter 11—can take a long, long time to do.

The point of this chapter is not to tell you *don't use materials designed for English learners*.

Again, good materials are not only great, they're better. They allow you to learn faster, with less effort. But be careful of the materials you use. Always ask yourself, *are these materials high-quality?* If the answer is no, don't use them.

You also have to ask yourself, *is what I'm learning natural and helping me to learn the* right *chunks and bits of English?* For example, if you're learning conversation, are your materials teaching you conversational English? Newspaper English, for example, is very different from conversation so learning from newspapers won't help you to speak better.

Make sense?

Good.

On the last point: the difference between newspapers and conversational English. There isn't space to talk about this in detail here, and it's much easier to do visually.

So I've created a free training that summarises some of the points from this book, and includes data and graphs that visualise the difference between conversation and newspapers.

You can get it here: https://doingenglish.com/freetraining.

**CHAPTER 10**

**FANTASTIC FLUENCY**

Before we start this chapter, I need to give you a warning: *There's a good chance you've skipped to this chapter without reading the rest of the book.*

Big mistake.

Yes, yes, I know: fluency is a sexy topic.

But what we talk about here builds on what we've *already* talked about in the previous chapters. And in fact, if you've taken on board the ideas from previous chapters (you're learning with the 'Two-Track Approach', considering the LKC Triangle as a whole, you're learning in chunks and starting with high quality, natural English m materials), you're *already building fluency faster than ever before.*

What we talk about in this chapter will help speed up the process. But only if you've got the base right, first.

So, if you have skipped here… go back.

### What Is Fluency, Exactly?

Imagine walking along the road outside your house. It's the same road you always walk along. You don't need to think about it… in fact, you're not aware of the road at all. The chances are you're thinking about something completely different. Daydreaming about the hot girl or guy you met the other day. Your favourite band. Or whatever it is that floats your boat.

Now imagine being in a foreign city that you've never been to before. New sights, sounds, lights… people everywhere. Noise. Chaos. Cars whizzing by, shop signs that you can't read.

This is a different experience to walking around outside your home. You're disorientated, confused – hyper-aware of everything around you.

Anybody who has spent time walking around new cities—especially cities like Tokyo or Hong Kong—will know how invigorating this is. But also how exhausting it can be.

The first time I went to Tokyo, I was constantly confused and lost.

Everything looked the same. I couldn't find my way around.

There are lights, sounds, people everywhere. It's a totally different experience to the British countryside where I grew up.

Well, fluency is like being on the road outside your home. And the second situation is disfluency.

Your brain works like this for a very good reason: to conserve energy. It shuts out everything that it doesn't consciously need to think about. And only lets in the information it most needs. It also automates common tasks. So, when it comes to being somewhere new, well… your brain doesn't know what is important and what isn't. So it lets everything in.

This is what makes you feel confused and disoriented. As you become familiar with the area, you store an automated route that you always follow. Turn left here. Walk straight. Turn right at the end of the road. You also block out irrelevant information (for example, a yellow car that's always there).

It's the same with English.

We're aiming to be "fluent" in the streets of English. So fluent that we can walk around and get where we need to go without thinking about it.

When you're not familiar with a language, you're consciously aware of what you want to say. Because of this, you have to calculate how to say something in your head, which is hard. Nothing is automated. And there is a mess of things going on at once. This is why you feel confused and disoriented.

Incidentally, this is also why saying unnatural, "non-chunked" things stands out to native speakers. *"Could you aid me in this task?"* (vs *"Could you help me with this?"*) is like a big, strange, black car with blacked-out windows parked on the street where they live. It's new. It's unexpected. And it grabs their attention and forces them to notice and consciously process it.

### What's Happening in Your Brain?

There's another reason why the metaphor of roads is very appropriate. You actually have "roads" in your brain.

Well, kind of.

They're not actually roads.

They're pathways.

*Neural* pathways.

The brain is made up of billions and billions of neurons. These are little cells which fire pulses of electricity at each other. Thought and consciousness emerge from the patterns that these little pulses make.

OK, yes, I realise that's an extreme simplification.

And also remember: when it comes to the brain, nobody really knows much for sure – the brain is largely a mystery even today. But you get the basic idea.

What all this means is, when you say a phrase in English, a group of neurons fire information at each other in a pattern. They connect. And the more often they connect, the stronger the connection becomes… until eventually that path becomes fixed in memory.

Imagine you use a phrase such as *'a lot of the…'* again and again. Each time, you connect the same path of neurons until eventually it becomes a single fixed path. It becomes like your route home from work: now you can travel that path automatically.

Ok, so this is all rather complicated. But you don't really need to know this to get fluent in English. I'm telling you because I really want you to understand how important chunks are for fluency.

Chunks are a *language habit*.

And habits are just automated routines in the brain. A habit is an action that you have taken so many times that a permanent pathway is created in the brain, and now that action runs on autopilot.

The point is, the first step to building fluency is learning the right stuff. You can make bad habits just as easily as you can make good habits. We'll talk about accuracy and naturalness in detail in the next chapter. But right now, understand that all accuracy and naturalness are is good language habits. And also remember it's possible to be fluent in mistaken, unnatural English – so be careful what you learn and practise, as I discussed at length in the previous chapter.


### How Do We Build Fluency, FAST?

Have you ever done any weight training?

If you have, you already know how to build fluency in English.

When I started working with my personal trainer, Phil, I was amazed by the similarity between the advice he gave me and the advice I give my students.

Then I realised: language is a muscle just like any other. So it makes sense muscle is built in the same way that fluency is.

There's a term in fitness called "progressive overload". Put simply, to build muscle you have to overload the muscle. Say you're lifting a weight, and your limit is 10 repetitions.

The first 9 reps don't really do much. It's the final rep that forces your muscle to break and expand past its current capabilities. That's when you feel the "burn."

By overloading the muscle, you force it to grow so that it can manage the new load. Do this often enough, and over time the muscle gets bigger and stronger.

Soon, you'll find 10 reps with the same weight doesn't do anything. The exercise is now too easy. Overload doesn't happen.

So what do you do?

You've got to overload the muscle *more*.

You could take the same weight and lift it 20 times. But very quickly that's going to be too easy, too – until you need to lift the weight hundreds of times to get the same effect.

Surely there's a better way?

There certainly is, ma petite fleur.

Lift a heavier weight.

Now you can overload the muscle and force it to grow again with just 10 reps.

But of course, soon that weight won't be heavy enough, either, and it will be time to increase the weight again. This is what is known as "progressive overload". And building your fluency is exactly the same.

As a beginner, you learned and improved fast. This is because your fluency muscle was weak, and it didn't take much to make it grow. But over time, as you got better, the things you were doing became less and less effective. Until you reached the intermediate stage. Suddenly you found the way you were practising English wasn't really helping you improve anymore. It's like you've been lifting a weight that's far, far too light for you, hundreds and hundreds of times.

So now you need to switch to a *heavier weight* – an exercise that will apply greater intensity on your brain and work faster and better.

Incidentally, conversation schools use this to sell their "conversation lessons" very effectively.

*"Just chat with a native speaker,"* they say, *"and you'll get fluent."*

They offer you a free trial lesson, and the first time you go, everything is new and exciting: Wow! Speaking to a real live native speaker! You're nervous, and let's be honest, scared shitless of saying something stupid. You really want him or her to think your English is great. This is a very intense, high-pressure situation – which is very good practise. BUT – the thing that makes it intense is not speaking with a native… it's the fear factor.

Two or three lessons later?

You're completely comfortable with your new teacher. You no longer feel the fear. And so you no longer get any benefit from chatting with that person. It's like your weights have become too light, and now you need a heavier one.

Once you reach the intermediate level, conversation teachers and "partners" are hideously ineffective for most people.

But don't worry.

There's a better way.

### The Fear Factor

You've probably never heard of Danny Way.

I never had.

He's a skateboarder. And he was the first person to jump the Great Wall of China on a skateboard. Not only did he jump it, but he jumped it on a broken ankle which he smashed it up on the practise run.

Why do people do things like this?

It's hard to say.

I couldn't do it.

And I don't want to try.

But then, I'm not interested in extreme sports.

For the people who are into extreme sports, however… it's *succeed or die*. There is no other option.

If you go on YouTube and type in "on the roofs," you'll find videos by Vitaliy Raskalov & Vadim Makhorov. They're two Russian guys who climb stuff. Check out the video of them climbing the Shanghai Tower. No safety equipment, nothing.

Frankly, just watching their videos makes me feel physically sick. I hate—and I mean HATE—heights! But this situation is a perfect example of performance pressure. One wrong move… and you're dead. There's no two ways about it. Nobody is going to survive falling off the top of the Shanghai Tower.

The body protects itself in this kind of situation by triggering what's known as a "flow state." Flow state is a neurochemical cocktail of hormones pumped into the brain to increase awareness. Flow also increases creativity and problem-solving skills. In a nutshell, Flow state happens to keep the body alive in dangerous situations.

Now, you're probably not going to die if you make a mistake with your English. But you should think about it in the same way. There is no giving up. Just do it! Or fail trying. (In *Star Wars*, when Luke Skywalker lamely says, "OK… I'll give it a try," Yoda tells him: "No! Try not! Do! Or do not! There is no try.")

The more afraid you are of doing something in English, the more you stand to gain.

One of the best books I've read is Steven Kotler's *The Rise of Superman: Decoding the Science of Ultimate Human Performance*.

Read it.

The majority of the book is about extreme sports athletes—people just like Danny Way—and the science behind Flow state.

Well, guess what?

In Flow state, you learn and build skills faster and more effectively, too. Including speaking English.

As part of the EES members programme, I regularly interview experts from all kinds of industries (I call this the "Extraordinary English Conversations" series, or EECs for short). Last year, I interviewed Richard Graham, from "Genki English". Richard specialises in English education for primary schools, and he's learned several languages to fluency.

One of those languages is French. In the interview, Richard told me about when he was a teenager learning French. He was in France on holiday with his family, and his father fell sick. He had to be rushed to hospital for open-heart surgery. The doctors didn't speak English. Nobody in Richard's family spoke French. In fact, Richard was the only one who knew *any* French at all – and suddenly he had to get good enough to communicate with the doctors. It really was a life-or-death situation.

The result?

He got very good at French, very quickly.

Another example that Richard gave is going on live TV to debate politics…in Japanese. He originally went on there to join a simple talk show, but then got invited to discuss politics. Again, this was a very high-pressure situation – there was a very high risk of major embarrassment.

The result?

He got good at Japanese really, really quickly.

Now, it's unlikely that you will find yourself in these exact situations. I certainly hope you never find yourself in the situation where a loved one has to have open-heart surgery in an English-speaking country… or anywhere else, for that matter. But it would be really good for improving your English! The point is: *you can and should figure out how to engineer the same kind of pressure, the same kind of high intensity, into your everyday learning.*

This by itself isn't enough, of course.

You also need that solid Two-Track routine of learning combined with your using English as much as you can. Adding in using English in high-pressure situations is then like putting your English improvement on steroids. But you do need the learning, too. Otherwise your growth will be slow – you'll build fluency, yes, but only in what you've learned. Go back to Chapter 4 for this.

## CHAPTER 11

## SPEAKING ACCURATELY AND NATURALLY

EVERYBODY SAYS they want to be more fluent in English. But just being fluent is not enough. Shit English said fast is still shit English.

Alongside building fluency, you also need to work on building accuracy and "naturalness".

First though, let me repeat what I said in the previous chapter: **if you've skipped here without reading the previous chapters (especially Chapter 4, and Chapter 6 on chunking), you're wasting your time**. On the other hand, if you've done everything else well, building naturalness is actually pretty easy.

What I talk about here simply speeds up the process.

It's like taking an already excellent sports car and fitting it with better tires – but of course, just having the tires without the car is pointless.

## *What Is Accuracy and Naturalness?*

We said that *fluency* is like walking along the road outside your house. It's knowing the roads so well you can just walk, drive or cycle along them without having to think about it.

*Disfluency*, on the other hand, is like being in a foreign city where everything is new, and you're disoriented and confused and you don't know where you're going and you're hyper-aware of everything going on around you.

We can continue this metaphor here. Speaking with naturalness and accuracy is like being familiar with the roads, but also knowing what is the quickest, most efficient route from Point A to Point B.

A great example of this: I often used to cycle to my mother-in-law's house when I was still living in Japan. My mother-in-law lived on completely the opposite side of Tokyo to me, and it's about a 25-kilometre bike ride. But it's a fairly easy route and only took me about an hour.

I could go this fast because it's basically straight all the way. But I didn't *have* to take that route. I could have taken a completely different route if I wanted to. I could have started by cycling in the opposite direction, going all the way around the city. That's not an efficient route, though. Sure. It'd get me there. And I could "practise" that route until I know it so well I don't have to think about it. With practise, I'd even get faster. But it'd still be a crappy route to take.

Speaking with naturalness and accuracy is using the shortest, most efficient way to communicate the things that you want to say. And this means speaking in native-like chunks.

What does and does not sound natural is not logical. "Pleasant first half of the day to you!" is perfectly grammatical. Only it sounds weird, because the chunk we *expect* in this situation is "Good morning".

Naturalness is all to do with people's expectations. People expect common, high-frequency, highly predictable chunks.

Remember what I said about the human brain? It's lazy and desperately wants to save as much energy as possible. In conversation, chunks help you, the speaker, to speak fluently. They are automatic and don't need to be constructed from grammar rules and individual words. This makes them very, very efficient. Your brain can just pull them out of memory and use them, as they are, ready to go. The analogy I used in Chapter 6 is they're like language 'shortcut-keys'. Instead of constructing what you need to say manually, you hit the shortcut-key, and it's processed automatically and instantly.

This is exactly the same for the listener. When someone is listening to you, they are able to understand you by accessing the chunks already stored in their memory; that is, they're also hitting those shortcut-keys.

If you speak in natural chunks, people can understand you instantly without making any special effort.

For example, if you ask a native speaker to complete the phrase: *"At the end of the _____ "*, everyone knows it's "day", although "night", "road" or even "snake's tail" are also perfectly grammatical. "At the end of the day" is a chunk – the others are not.

Also recall that even if you pronounced the "end" but wrong—say, "ond"—it would still sound natural and fluent. On the other hand, pronouncing a chunk like this as individual words forces the listener to hear it as individual words – which makes it much harder to understand.

## What Grammar Really Is

Grammar didn't come first – language did.

One day, some clever people called "linguists" sat down and analysed the language they heard. They tried to pull out patterns and make rules to explain the language.

They did an OK job.

Probably they did the best job they could. But it's not very good, to be honest. First, there are too many exceptions. No rule describes everything, so there are always some things that don't fit. Second, native speakers don't always speak "correctly" according to the rules of grammar. Third, language is so complex that it's difficult to explain grammar in a way that's useful for people learning the language. Fourth, a lot of recent research suggest those grammar rules don't even exist in your head (there are different theories and different arguments – I won't go into them here, as it's too complex for this book, but ask me in the bar sometime).

Grammar rules can be useful.

I'm not denying that.

But **only** when you use them in the right way.

Unfortunately, as we already talked about in Chapter 6, the way most schools teach languages is totally backwards. They start with grammar rules, teach you individual words, and then expect you to be able to speak.

Remember: always start with samples of real, natural English and work up. Read or listen to your materials and get the basic idea, as a whole. Then you can take it apart, notice and learn the chunks, analyse the grammar and look up some vocabulary words. Never do it in the opposite direction: don't start with individual words and grammar rules.

Again, don't misunderstand me: studying grammar rules *can* be useful. You've just got to use them in the right way. Use them to understand the language that you hear real people speaking; use them to notice things about English. Really, the best time to study grammar is to deepen your knowledge when you already speak fluently and naturally – just like a native speaker does when they study grammar at school.

Now, there is a problem with have to deal with here: the way native speakers use language (especially in speaking) isn't always grammatical, as I mentioned.

Here's an example… a controversial one.

I once sent an email—one of my free daily emails; see the back of this book—where I wrote "there's people". A blatant grammar mistake. Tsk tsk. Bad boy Julian. Yes, I know.

In reply, someone sent me an email saying:

> Mistake: There's no people outside
> Correction: There are no people outside

Yes, I should be more careful.

Perhaps.

A mistake is a mistake.

But there is an interesting lesson here. Interesting, but again, controversial. So read this with an open mind, OK?

In your grammar book you would have learnt to use the verb *is* before or after a singular noun, and *are* before or after plural nouns.

So not "There is people", but "There are people".

Right?

Well yes... kind of.

That is the "correct" usage, yes, according to your grammar book. But if you look at real language that real people speak, you'll find out some very interesting things about this "incorrect" chunk of English.

You see, native speakers rarely speak like grammar books say they should. In fact, a lot of the time they don't speak in a grammatical way at all.

I looked up "there's people" in a huge data bank of American English, and compared it with the grammatically 'correct' phrase "there're people".

Guess what I found? That's right – *"There's people"* is significantly more frequent than "there're people".

So I looked it up again in a data bank of British English.

Guess what? Again, we see the same pattern: the incorrect "there's people" is significantly more common.

So although, yes, "there're people" is correct according to grammar books...in reality? It's only correct in grammar books. Because it doesn't reflect the way people actually use English. Put simply, here the ungrammatical, "mistaken" chunk is more common, easier to say and easier to understand.

Is the phrase "there's people" *really* a mistake?

I would say NO.

Now, don't misunderstand me. I'm not saying you should learn "incorrect English". I still advise you to learn the grammatically correct version – "there're people".

But the point I want to make is this: **don't assume that the grammar rules you learn are perfect and always right**. Doing that will leave you very frustrated, because in the real world you're going to see lots of examples that don't match the rules.

Also don't assume you know better or that you are definitely right. Living and working in Japan, I occasionally came across people who couldn't do anything useful with their English, but had a weird pride about their grammatical knowledge. They loved to every opportunity to humiliate native speakers with it (especially English teachers, to whom they love to say things like, "If you're a teacher, why don't you know this?!"). This is small-minded stupidity at its best. And totally pointless.

Grammar rules are *never* simply 'right' or 'wrong'. They should be understood and used flexibly – as *guidelines* for understanding language.

A good example of this is Wendy. At the time she was a MEFA student. Now she's a fully-fledged member of my Extraordinary English speakers group. Anyway, Wendy is an English teacher herself, and she asked me how she can improve her usage of tenses.

"I said to my students, *'Did you do your homework?'*, but then I realised, *'Have you done your homework?'* is correct!"

Which confused me.

Because I would also say, "Did you do your homework?".

And indeed, after a bit of research so would most native speakers – it's not only perfectly, appropriate and natural sounding, it's a very high-frequency way of expressing this.

Perhaps the grammar book says, "have you done..." is better. But the grammar book isn't real. The way people actually speak, is.

The point is, always check your intuitions. They might be wrong. And indeed, if you used badly designed materials to learn from previously, your intuitions are probably screwed up (see Chapter 9).

There are several exercises and tools I teach my MEFA students for checking—and changing—their intuitions. It wouldn't be practical to demonstrate them in written form, neither is there space. But you can find information on the course at the end of this book, if you're interested.

But if you're not going to focus on grammar… what should you focus on instead?

Meaning.

Read or listen to samples of language that real people use. Begin your study by trying to understand *the meaning* of the sample as a whole. Then understand the blocks of meaning (chunks), and how they're used. If you really, really want to, you can use then use grammar rules and a dictionary to help you understand the details later. Though personally I'd just skip this stage.

### The Big "N" of Naturalness

There was a house on the street corner near where I used to live. I walked past that house every day for years and years.

One day, the house was gone.

I went away for the weekend, and when I walked past on Monday morning, the corner was just a patch of bare ground. The house had totally vanished.

This isn't unusual in Tokyo. Houses go up and come down fast. They're made of wood, and it doesn't take much to knock them down.

The strange thing is though…*no matter how hard I think now, I can't for the life of me remember what that house looked like.*

What colour were the walls?

What kind of door did it have?

What shape was the roof?

I walked past it for years! But I can't remember.

Why?

Because I never actually paid attention to that house. It was there, in the background. But I never really *noticed* it. Not until it was gone, anyway.

Speaking naturally is all about noticing things. Noticing how natives speak, and what is—and is not—natural. Noticing how you speak, and what is—and is not—natural.

The best way to do this is the Two Track Approach. Learning and using done in balance.

### *Should you have people fix your mistakes?*

When it comes to the (incorrect) ways you approach learning and speaking English, the fastest way is to have an expert coach you through the process. This is what I do, and it's how my business makes good money.

A while ago I read an interesting story about Coca-Cola. I don't know if it's true (it sounds like an urban myth to me), but it illustrates a good point.

In 1886, John Pemberton invented Coca-Cola... then two years later, he died. A guy called Asa Candler bought the rights to Coca-Cola and worked hard marketing it. Soon it became a popular drink. But not as popular as it could be.

At that time Coca-Cola was sold as a syrup to shops, who then mixed it and sold cupped drinks.

One day a man walked into the Coca-Cola office and said, *"I can teach you how to double the company's profits overnight. If you want my advice, it will cost you $5000,"* he said.

That was a huge amount of money at the time. But Candler paid it. In return, he got a slip of paper with two words written on it: "Bottle it". And that, apparently, is how Coca-Cola started to be sold in bottles.

The point is this: sometimes the biggest breakthroughs are extremely simple, plain, and…well, kind of obvious. But it often takes another person with fresh eyes to *notice* them.

Candler was so focused on selling more syrup to shops that he didn't notice the obvious alternative: why not sell bottles of the drink straight to consumers?

Similarly, you probably make the same mistakes with your English again and again and again. And you have no idea you're doing it. You're probably so focused on a certain aspect of English that you miss the obvious breakthrough. For example, you're convinced people can't understand you because of your accent, so you spend all your time trying to improve your accent. Never realising the real reason they can't understand you is because your English is messy and disorganised, or because your ideas simply don't make sense.

Spotting these problems is what I excel at.

And absolutely, yes, you should try to get this kind of feedback.

But what about getting someone to "fix your mistakes"?

Honestly, this is far less useful…

Sometimes getting feedback on your English speaking can be helpful, yes. But only if they know HOW to give you good feedback. But the average native speaker doesn't.

You see it all the time: the person doing the corrections just wants to get it done fast or doesn't really know what is wrong with your English. So they fix your grammar. But what you said still sounds weird, unnatural… and may not even make sense. And worse; you now believe it's good English, because a "native speaker" corrected it.

I'm not going to name any specific sites, because it's not fair to slag off other businesses in my book. But there are quite a few social-media style websites and services where you can submit something written in English and have other users correct your mistakes.

It's a good idea, and it sounds great… but it isn't.

I used to use one such website and get loads of corrections on my Japanese – which felt great! But then my wife would look at the corrections people gave me and say: *"That sounds strange…!"*

You see, the problems I had (and which most people have) were usually "higher level" problems. It's a higher level problem when we say something unnatural, weird, or culturally inappropriate. Or when we say something that makes no sense. But most people who give corrections only give quick, low-level grammar corrections. They ignore the real, high-level problems which are much harder to correct.

Ultimately, you learn nothing valuable from the process. Yes, you get back something that's grammatical… but just correcting the grammar of a sentence doesn't make it a good sentence. Weird English constructed grammatically is still weird English.

"Have a good first half of the day!" is grammatically correct, but it sure sounds weird. In this case, you need to learn the equally grammatical but much more natural chunk: "Good morning!".

A much better way is to "correct" your mistakes is to do what we've already talked about extensively in this book: work with a balance of focused, intensive study to grow your English fast, then use and expose your-self to English as much as you can in a natural, *not-study-time* way. As you do this, your awareness of how English should sound will grow. And if you combine this with reflection on your own English, you will start to spot the things which are different.

Also, once you start learning and speaking in chunks, many mistakes fix themselves: if you struggle with prepositions or those tricky little words like "a" and "the", learning in chunks makes your job significantly easier.

This isn't just my opinion.

Occasionally I review academic papers – about the only thing I do on a volunteer basis, because I enjoy it.

You might already know, but in scientific publishing an author submits a research paper to a journal, and it then needs to be reviewed by two or three people, who make a decision about whether the research is good enough to be published. It's all anonymous (well, it's supposed to be... some people give them-selves away) and this ensures top quality.

About a week ago, I reviewed a paper by an author who did a study of function word mistakes in Korean

English learners. Things like, "a", "the" and "of". Yes, those pesky, tricky little words all English learners struggle with.

The author looked specifically at chunks and mistakes made as a part of them (and almost all function words are actually a part of a chunk because that's their job). The conclusion from the research was quite simple – the best way to stop making mistakes with these tricky little words is to learn in chunks right from the start. People make mistakes because they're over-focused on words and rules.

Instead, you should be focused on chunks and learning chunks. Not words. Not rules. Chunks.

If you do this?

Suddenly something which seemed impossible and extremely complicated to learn becomes dead simple… and your problems slowly disappear over time.

### Julian's Favourite English Learning Exercise

One of the best exercises for improving your listening skill and also noticing things about English—i.e. building your intuition—is "dictation".

You'll need a short English conversation—two to three minutes long is best—and a transcript you can use to check your version with later (important: don't look at the transcript yet).

All you've got to do is listen to the conversation and write out everything you hear. Pause as often as you need to. Rewind the audio listening to difficult sections as many times as you need. Repeat the whole audio several times, if you need.

For most people a two to three-minute audio is going to take between 15 and 30 minutes to complete. This is a slow exercise, and that's *why* it works so well: it will force your listening skills, but also get you noticing features of English you weren't aware of before.

Dictation forces you to pay attention to every little sound. You can't write what you can't hear, after all. You'll also never learn what you don't notice, and often, when it comes to those tricky little words like 'a' and 'the', you probably never even hear them. Well, with dictation this will become really obvious when you finish and check your dictation with the original version. You'll see right away where you've gone wrong, and what you've missed. Pay special attention to the chunks of language, and the crushed-down sound of them.

Remember: chunks are pronounced in single units, and the key to mastering prepositions and other kinds of small function words is learning them in chunks.

## CHAPTER 12

## EFFECTIVE SPEAKING MADE
## DEAD SIMPLE

THIS BOOK ISN'T for people who want to speak English well. It's for people who want to be outstanding.

*Extraordinary.*

In order to do that, we need to go beyond English.

I often hear students say: "My goal is to speak English like a native speaker." But although native speakers do speak English fluently without having to give it much thought, they are not necessarily outstanding speakers. To be honest, they may not even be *good* speakers.

This should be obvious from the fact that you need three things to speak English well – not just the Language, but also Knowledge of your topic, and sensitivity to the Culture.

Now I want to introduce you to a slightly different way of thinking about this. This is a set of guidelines, or principles, which you can use to present yourself to the world, through English, for the maximum result.

Many native speakers have no idea how to do any of this.

These principles have served as very effective guidelines for me in any kind of communicative situation or any situation where I need to make decisions, whether it's in my business or in my personal life. It doesn't matter whether I'm having a conversation with someone one-on-one, whether I'm talking to people as part of a group, whether I am talking to a group—as in a presentation or a speech—whether I'm making a video to go on my YouTube channel, or a session for one of my courses or a coaching call.

In a nutshell, it is: be Empathetic, Authentic, and Relentless in our pursuit of outstanding English.

Here's how I explain it:

---

Be Empathetic: Always show empathy and understanding for other people. This means: aim to truly understand the people you interact with, the people in your life, the groups of people that you associate with. Ask people questions, listen to people, try to learn everything you can about them. Study human psychology, the human condition. Watch people. Watch how they act, and how they behave. Learn as much as you can about people.

Be Authentic and true to yourself: Share your full self with the world – not just the things that you're confident and comfortable with, but also the things that you're *not* confident about, and the things you're *un*comfortable with. Share these things with the world, anyway. Don't worry about the opinions of other people – the people who are not like you, who are fundamentally different from you. Forget about them, ignore them. Concentrate all of your time and energy on the people who matter to you. The people who are important to you. Form strong, authentic relationships with those people.

Be Relentless: Keep pushing forward in the pursuit of excellence. Never give in when you know something truly matters. Never be satisfied with half-assed efforts and mediocre results. Be the best, have the best, and do the best.

———

Now let's discuss these three points in detail and talk about how they can serve you in your life.

### Who Are You Talking To?

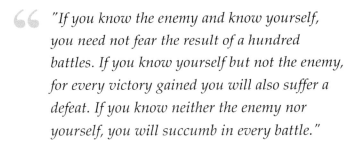

"If you know the enemy and know yourself, you need not fear the result of a hundred battles. If you know yourself but not the enemy, for every victory gained you will also suffer a defeat. If you know neither the enemy nor yourself, you will succumb in every battle."

— — SUN TZU, THE ART OF WAR

———

You already know this by now, but a long time ago I was a secondary school teacher in Japan. In any class, there are always trouble students – the ones who don't listen, who talk back, and who generally make their teacher's life difficult.

Sometimes you'll come across students who *really* have problems. Many teachers—especially foreign English teachers—sadly don't deal with those students well.

They tell them things like: *"You need English for your future,"* and in some cases they get angry and shout at students. But they never think to ask *why* a student misbehaves.

Well, I asked why.

And I can tell you…the answers I got (normally from the child's homeroom teachers, not from the students themselves) were pretty fucking scary.

There are children in schools who have serious problems at home. Their dad beats them. Their mum brings strange men home every night. There are girls who are scared of being raped by step-fathers and boys who are abused every day.

And teachers mindlessly tell them to concentrate on their English? Yeah, right. Like that's going to happen.

The point is, you can't deal effectively with a problem —whether it's a problem student or a difficult business deal—until you have all the information.

You need to take the time to understand the people you work with. So when in doubt, shut up and listen.

There's an old cliché that my grandmother often used to repeat: *"You have two ears and one mouth – use them in that proportion."* That means: Spend twice as much time listening as you do talking.

One of the best ways to avoid making mistakes, or sounding daft when you speak, is to listen instead. Ironically, people who spend more time listening are considered better speakers by the people they spend time with… and there's a very good reason for this. First, people like to be listened to. More importantly though, people who listen to others understand people better – and when you understand someone, you're able to communicate much more effectively.

You've probably met people in your life whom you like talking to just because they seem to *understand* you. It's like they understand what you want to say, even without your having to say it. There's a connection. This means that person has *empathy* for you.

Aim to be that kind of person: the one other people feel they connect with.

The dictionary defines 'empathy' as:

*"The ability to understand and share the feelings of another."*

Become a student of people.

Aim to understand people on a deep level. Really listen to the people you interact with on a regular basis.

This is especially important in sales situations.

A great example of this is one that you've probably experienced yourself: going into a clothing shop. Not long ago, I was shopping for a new jacket. In the first shop I went into, the assistant recommended a jacket without even asking me anything. He told me it would suit me… but in what situation? Who knows. This jacket was also clearly one they were trying hard to sell. There was a display right in front of the shop, and all the main displays included this jacket.

Clearly he wanted to sell the jacket for his own reasons; he didn't really care who bought it, or whether it was the right thing to buy.

His final attempt was to tell me: "Your colleagues at work will be really jealous when they see you in this jacket!"

Big mistake.

First, I'm self-employed and don't have any colleagues. Second, even if I did, I wouldn't give a shit what they thought.

Now, compare this to shop number two. There, the assistant asked me a few questions – where would I wear the jacket? What purpose was it for?

I told him I make online courses and work online coaching people to speak amazing English.

The jacket he recommended wasn't one I would have picked myself. It was navy blue, and made of a rough, but fine wool with a slight sheen. Great under strong studio lights. It's also very fitted, he explained, because jackets tend to look wider than they really are on camera, especially when you're sitting down.

I bought the jacket, and I love it.

So whereas shop assistant number one just irritated the hell out of me, shop assistant number two sold me a fairly expensive jacket.

All because he took the time to ask me a couple of questions and because he listened to what I wanted.

Speaking well is about *strategy*, not *tactics*. In sales, someone who uses *tactics* is trying to turn every single encounter into a sale – right here, right now. But someone who uses a *strategy* is looking at the bigger picture – trying to develop good relationships with people over the long term. The first sales assistant was all about tactics. The second had a strategy. Even if I didn't buy a jacket that time, it's the kind of store I would go back to again and again, because of the way he treated me.

Every time I ever rented an apartment in Tokyo—we moved three times in the years I was there—I always got the same line from the realtor: *"I shouldn't tell you this, but there was another couple who came to look at this same apartment today, and I think they're going to take it."*

Total bullshit.

Compare that with the realtor who sat down with us over a coffee, got all our details, then called back *two months* later because he'd found a place he thought we'd like. Ultimately, we decided the place was a little small for us and didn't take it, but the point is: this realtor had a very clear (and effective) strategy.

He knew we wouldn't find something quickly, so he didn't bother wasting our time with things that weren't right for us, or with fake pressure tactics. Instead, he waited for something that actually was right for us, and he showed us that.

Business, marketing, sales, speaking English well – it's all about people. The better you understand people, the better you'll be.

There are so many people in the world who want to speak "intelligent" or "sophisticated" English. They spend all their time memorising clever-sounding words, then they try to use them whenever they can, hoping to impress people. That's a tactic. And not a very good one. They never take the time to understand the person they're talking to, so more often than not they just seem weird, not intelligent.

One of the best ways to understand people is simply *to ask questions*. Ask people things. Learn about the people that you talk to and interact with – not just the new people that you meet, but the people you've known all your life. Ask them things, try to learn new things about those people all the time. Ask them questions and then sit back, shut up and just listen.

### Who Are You?

In 2007, two Scottish guys launched a brewing business that would transform the beer industry in the UK.

James Watt, co-founder of BrewDog, put some of their home-brewed beer into a Tesco (a British supermarket) competition. Shortly after, they got a phone call telling them they'd won first, second, third and fourth prize. Not only that, but Tesco wanted to roll out their beer – 2,000 cases a week.

Tesco had no idea BrewDog consisted of just two people who were hand-filling bottles from a tent, with their dog. But in just a couple of years, BrewDog grew to become one of the fastest-growing food and drink companies in the UK, with more than 500 employees, 44 bars worldwide, and a turnover in excess of £20 million in 2013.

How did they do it?

First of all, pure guts.

But much more than that. BrewDog didn't just create a product. They created an entire *culture*.

They broke all the rules.

The beer BrewDog makes is totally different from any other beer you can buy. And their way of doing business is totally different from any other, too.

BrewDog are punks of the beer world and they've created a brand that is totally unique and resonates with the right kind of people for them.

On one level, being yourself—being authentic—seems quite simple. Just be yourself. However, when you really think about what it means to be authentic, you start to realise that it's actually quite an elusive idea – it's quite hard to pin down exactly what it means to be authentic.

Being authentic means being confident and comfortable with yourself, and confident and comfortable sharing yourself to the outside world. **Not just the good things.** But everything. It means being comfortable and confident with being vulnerable, showing the less positive aspects of yourself. The things that you are not so proud of. It means being comfortable saying, *"I was wrong, I made a mistake, I'm not perfect, I don't know everything, I am still learning, I make mistakes."*

It also means not doing things just because other people think you should.

My work is a perfect example.

Many of the people I work with in my coaching groups use English in the world of international business, whether they are employed by a company or they own the company.

The biggest mistake most business English teachers make when they market themselves is putting on a suit and trying to fit in with the "corporate" image they imagine their clients have.

If that's how they're truly comfortable… then fine. But I look stupid in a suit and tie, and nothing—and I mean nothing—would get me to carry one of those horrible leather briefcases that most businessmen carry.

I'm pretty casual in the way I present myself, and the way I speak – I'm not afraid to say *shit, fuck* and *bollocks* in front of my clients.

I've got tattoos and pierced ears and am far more likely to be wearing boots and a leather jacket than so-called 'professional' wear.

In short, just like BrewDog are totally different from any other brewing company in the UK, I'm totally different from what you'd expect a *business English* teacher to be.

And that's exactly why I make a lot more money than your average English teacher. Because I've got guts, and I'm not afraid to show my full personality. I appeal to just the right people and let everyone who doesn't like me fuck off.

Ultimately, people do business with people they know, like, and trust. And intuitively we don't trust people who try to be something they're not. But here's the important thing: not everybody likes me. Quite the opposite, in fact. Lots of people *don't* like me. My YouTube channel gets as many negative—sometimes quite abusive—comments as it does positive. And that's a good thing.

There's a concept in marketing known as "polarization." Political campaign planners are masters of polarisation. A fantastic example is the whole Brexit mess in the UK, with the UK leaving the European Union, and the run-up to that.

The campaigns from both parties took everybody from this vague, general middle and polarised them, splitting them into two very clear, very distinct groups. You were either in, or you were out.

People in one group absolutely could not understand the feelings and thinking of people in the other group.

Donald Trump did exactly the same thing.

So did Marmite with their "You either love it or you hate it" advertisements. And of course, so did Brew-Dog. Not everybody likes BrewDog beer – but the people who do, *love it*.

This is polarisation at its most extreme. But when you start to share your real self—and I mean ALL of your-self—you have the same effect on people.

Some people will be very strongly drawn to you, as if attracted by a super-powerful magnet. These people are people who are fundamentally like you. They're people similar to you. People who share the same values as you. People who have empathy for you. They're people who can accept you for who you truly are.

In the same way that a magnet can draw things towards it, when flipped over, a magnet also repels other things. So if you're authentic and true to your-self, some people are *not* going to like you. Some people will be pushed away, repelled. These are people who are fundamentally different from you. People who are not like you. People who do not share your ideals. People who cannot accept you for who you truly are.

The stronger the magnet is, the stronger the attraction will be. *And the stronger it will push other things away.*

You might think this is a bad thing. We don't want to be disliked, we don't want to be rejected. However, herein lies the problem: you can never please everyone, and when you try to, actually you please no one.

It's the difference between a person who has a small group of friends prepared to die for them, compared with another person who has hundreds of friends... but no one he can truly rely on.

There's a great scene in Nancy Meyers's film "The Intern". Ben—a retired 70-year-old—applies for an intern position. Right from the start, he's very careful about what he wears. Classic suits, attention to detail, and always with a handkerchief.

He gets the job, and people start to comment on his clothes.

"Hey Ben, you gonna wear a suit every day?"

"You bet," replies Ben.

"Confidence! I like how you roll," comes the reply.

The boss even tells him he doesn't need to dress up for the job: "Don't feel like you have to dress up... we're super casual here."

"I'm comfortable in a suit, thank you," again replies Ben.

Here's the thing though – Ben stands out.

He dresses well in an environment where everybody dresses super casual, and as a result he turns heads.

He is authentic, and true to himself… and doesn't change himself just because of what other people say.

Researchers at Harvard University did a study about fashion. More precisely, about how people perceive others based on the way they dress.

And the result? People who dress 'unusually' get a lot more respect than people who are 'well dressed'.

Lady Gaga is a perfect example.

Her fashion sense is very unusual, and it gets noticed. But also people like Steve Jobs and Mark Zuckerberg are perfect examples. CEOs of huge, major companies, you'd expect them to be sitting around "properly dressed." But while everyone else is at the meeting in their business suits... they're in jeans and t-shirts. Well, "was" in Jobs' case – he's not sitting around wearing anything, now. But you get the idea.

Another example is people who go to high-end fashion boutiques dressed in gym clothes. Shop assistants know these people are likely to spend a lot of money – and <u>not</u> the people who come "appropriately" dressed.

The message is clear – casual confidence impresses.

And you know what?

That's exactly the same with English, and the way you speak. The people who get the most success are the people who "wear" their English in a totally casual, comfortable, natural way.

This doesn't mean you have to be crazy like Lady Gaga, of course. It just means stop caring what people think of you. Be yourself and be comfortable with yourself. Stop apologising for your "bad English" or trying to speak with a native-accent so people don't realise you're a non-native and roll with what you've got – what is uniquely you.

When you do this, the quality of people you draw to you and your work will be much higher. And the people who aren't right for you… well, they can just fuck off, can't they.

## *Be Relentless*

Have you ever seen the film *Rocky*?

If you've never seen it, I highly recommend you go and watch it.

Written and acted by Sylvester Stallone, *Rocky* is one of the most successful films in history. But what a lot of people don't realise is the challenges and hardships that Stallone faced to make that film. When he first went to New York to become an actor, no one would hire him. He was so poor that he had to sleep in the New Jersey bus terminal.

This was the lowest point of Stallone's life. But one day he saw the boxer Muhammad Ali, and it gave him the idea for a story. He put pen to paper and wrote the script for the film *Rocky*.

Stallone took the script to a producer and was offered 125,000 dollars for it. But there was a condition: the producer said that he didn't want Stallone to act in the film. But he didn't want to be a screenwriter, he wanted to be an actor. So he refused.

Can you imagine that?

Here's this guy, completely broke, sleeping on the street and he's offered 125,000 dollars… but he refuses it.

A few weeks later, the producer comes back, and this time he offers Stallone 350,000 dollars – an incredible sum of money. But still he says Stallone can't act in the film. Stallone says, "No thank you."

Eventually the producer gives in and says that Stallone can act in the film, but he'll only pay 35,000 dollars – just 10 percent of what he previously offered. Stallone accepted, and the rest, as they say, is history.

The point of this story is that when you truly want something, don't let anything stop you. Be relentless in your pursuit of that goal. Never give up. Keep on trying. No matter how difficult things seem, no matter how many hardships and challenges you face, be relentless in the pursuit of the things that truly matter to you.

Stallone didn't want to be a screenwriter; he wanted to be an actor. The thing that truly mattered to him—his *Why*—was acting. He was relentless in the pursuit of his goal and was eventually successful *because* he was so relentless.

*Rocky* was the starting point of a very long, very successful career for Sylvester Stallone. Imagine if he'd given in and settled for the producer's first offer? Where would he be now?

The same attitude will serve you well when speaking English. Your English skills (or lack of them) should never, ever be an excuse not to do the things you know matter. If something seems hard, try anyway. And if it doesn't work? Ask what you need to do to improve yourself to *make* it work. But never—and I mean *never*—be satisfied with half-assed efforts and mediocre results.

Right back in the introduction to this book, I told you how I went to Japan. I had a job interview lined up for a great position at an art gallery in Harajuku, a fashionable part of Tokyo.

I was so sure I'd get the job, but I didn't. My Japanese wasn't good enough.

It's funny, but although I didn't realise it then, that wasn't the first time a second language had held me back and stopped me from doing the things I wanted to do. Remember what I told you in Chapter 1 about how I believed I *couldn't* learn a language? How I believed I wasn't talented at languages? Well, while I was in my second year at university, I was offered a chance to go to Switzerland for three months. I would study at a university there, all expenses paid. It was a once in a lifetime opportunity. But at the last minute, I turned it down.

I made all kinds of excuses as to why I couldn't go, but the reality was that I was *afraid*. I was scared of being in an environment where I couldn't speak the language.

There were so many times I wanted to quit Japanese, too. After I was turned down by the art gallery, I got a job as an assistant English teacher working in a school. I enjoyed the teaching, but I *hated* all the other work I had to do such as planning lessons with teachers and joining meetings.

I felt embarrassed about my bad Japanese. I felt humiliated almost every day. The other teachers were busy and always seemed annoyed at having to deal with me – the guy who couldn't speak their language properly. When I had to join meetings, I had lots of ideas, but I didn't understand what people were saying. I was afraid of saying something stupid, so I always just sat in silence, nodding and agreeing with everything if asked a question.

It would have been so easy to just give up and go back to England. But I'm so glad that I didn't. Because if I had… if I'd given up just like I gave up on Switzerland… I wouldn't have the life that I have now.

Once I realised why my Japanese wasn't improving—that I was putting all my time and energy into the wrong things—I improved, fast. A lot changed in my life for the better. I got a job in a Japanese company and eventually left to start my own business. For years I did everything in Japanese exactly the same as I would have done if I were living in the UK, doing everything in English – the language barriers that held me back for so long totally disappeared.

Since then my life has changed significantly, and Japanese isn't a big part of it any more. I still read in Japanese, watch films and occasionally catch up with my friends. But the point I'm trying to make here, is no matter how hard things seem now, they can get better. You've just got to keep pushing forward to improve and refuse to be satisfied with half-assed efforts and mediocre results.

## AFTERWARDS

Thank you for investing in *Master English FAST*, and for choosing to take your extraordinary journey to English mastery with me.

I realise this book has been somewhat of a rollercoaster ride, and that I've likely challenged (and hopefully destroyed) many of the beliefs you had about improving your English.

These uncomfortable truths can be really bloody painful, I know. But consider them growing pains. Ultimately, it's all for the best.

This said, the journey ain't over.

And it never will be.

When it comes to English, there will always be more to learn, and room to improve. Learning is a lifelong pursuit. It started the day you were born, and it will continue until the day you die.

As you know by now, I'm very critical of the traditional education systems. The saddest thing for me is when students finish school and say, "Great! No more study!!" When I hear this, I know school has failed them. Because the people who live truly fulfilling lives are eternal students.

The question now, of course, is what are you going to do with the information you've just read?

It's a sad fact that most people will read this book and then never do anything. From the moment I started teaching, I've been frustrated and disappointed again and again.

It's frustrating for me personally, because writing this book was hard work – just like producing courses and programmes is super hard work. Sure, it's nice to get your money in my bank account. Ultimately, the sales that come from this book, the courses I make, as well as fees from coaching clients, are what put food on my table, beer in my fridge and support three full-time salaries and two part-time. The money helps me live. But more than that, you know what drives me? My

*Why*? Hearing success stories from people just like you. Yes, I've heard many over the years. But I want to hear more.

So do me a favour: do the damn work. Implement what you've learned in this book, do something amazing, and let me know.

Cheers,

Dr Julian Northbrook

## SOME FREE RESOURCES

Here are some free resources to further help you on your journey to English mastery.

### The Master English FAST Audiobook

To get the audiobook via the Doing English Learnistic app, simply go this URL:

https://doeng.co/mef

Follow the instructions carefully.

If it is your first time accessing the Doing English App, you'll need to install it first (note: this app isn't available in any of the app stores – you need to use the link above). If you already have the app, the book will simply be added to your existing account.

**Important:** this audiobook is only available via the app, and you need a smartphone that's not older than my grandfather. If you don't have a smartphone and can't use the app, this is unavailable to you.

### *Doing English Daily Newsletter*

I write daily English tips emails, that you can subscribe to for free. Every day at around 8am Ireland time, a new email will hit your inbox packed with tips and ideas for speaking better English. This is also the best way to keep up to date with my new books and coaching courses – which I promote in every email.

Sign up here:

https://doingenglish.com/

## The Rocket Launch Method Training

For a summary of the key points from this book in video-format (which lets me visualise some things we talked about here).

Go to:

https://doingenglish.com/freetraining


## The Good Shadowing Guide

Shadowing is a great exercise for developing your rhythm, intonation and "chunking" skills when speaking English – but the way most people do it is wrong. This guide will show you how to use shadowing properly and make it work for you personally.

You can get it here:

https://doingenglish.com/shadowing

## THE IMPLEMENTATION COURSE

After I originally published this book in 2016, many people said they wanted more: to go deeper into some topics we discuss, and to get my personal help to customise what they've learned here in this book. That's why I created the "Master English *FAST* Accelerator" coaching course.

You don't need this course to implement what you've learned here.

But if you want to see the fastest results, and transform your English speaking in as little as 90 days, it may be for you. I've copied the "basic" information page from https://doingenglish.com/mefa below:

---

Here you can get the basic information quickly, and then if you think the course is right for you... join my free daily emails, and I'll give you the opportunity to get more information and then enrol

### *What is MEFA?*

MEFA is a 12-week group coaching course with weekly study and homework tasks designed to:

- Give you as big a boost in English-speaking proficiency, as possible over the 90-days.
- Get you totally clear about everything you need to do to keep improving with English in your real-life consistently and forever.

Each week's training session, homework task and the daily feedback from Julian is packed with actionable techniques to change the most important parts of your English as fast as possible. The weekly group coaching calls and support you get via the discussion group is designed to help you customise what you learn to you personally.

## *Requirements*

To be right for MEFA, you must meet the following requirements (if you don't meet all of these, there's no point in joining, or even in me sending you more information).

- You must be thick-skinned (I can't work with people who get offended at the slightest criticism).
- You must be able to listen to advice without letting your own (incorrect) opinions about learning English get in the way.
- You must have a real need for English (whether you use English now in work, daily life or have a clear future need – i.e., this is not for hobbyists).
- You must commit to finishing the course. Statistics show the average completion rate for online courses only between 5% and 15%... the completion rate for MEFA is currently 90%. Why? Because I'm extremely strict about requiring you to submit homework, on time, before the deadline. And if you fail to do the work (and don't have a good reason such as an emergency) I will not hide my displeasure.

Also, one more thing:

The MEFA course is not a magic pill that will transform your English simply by joining and doing nothing.

It takes time and work.

For the opportunity to join and more detailed information about everything we do in MEFA, first subscribe to my daily emails:

https://doingenglish.com/emails

**OTHER BOOKS BY JULIAN**

These books (apart from the ones which haven't been released yet) are all abatable on Amazon as Kindle and paperback books: https://author.to/JulianNorthbrook

## Quick 'N' Dirty English Learning Series

- Think English, Speak English
- Fearless Fluency
- Awesome Accent
- The Secrets of Structured Learning

### *For Non-native English Teachers*

- The Extraordinary English Teacher [coming soon]
- English Teaching Sales Machine [coming soon]

## BOOKS MENTIONED

Here is a list of the books mentioned in this book. They're all well worth reading:

- A Cognitive Approach to Language Learning – Peter Skehan
- The Culture Map – Erin Meyer
- The Rise of Superman: Decoding the Science of Ultimate Human Performance – Steven Kotler
- Start with Why: How Great Leaders Inspire Everyone to Take Action – Simon Sinek
- Reading the Oxford Dictionary: one man, one year, 21,730 pages – Ammon Shea
- The 80/20 Principle: The Secret to Achieving More with Less – Richard Koch

- 80/20 Sales and Marketing: The Definitive Guide to Working Less and Making More – Perry Marshall
- Harry Hole Series – Jo Nesbo
- Inspector Chen Cao Series – Qiu Xiaolong

Printed in Great Britain
by Amazon